INVESTIGATING, SEIZING AND CONFISCATING THE PROCEEDS OF CRIME

Michael Levi
Lisa Osofsky

POLICE RESEARCH GROUP
CRIME DETECTION AND PREVENTION SERIES: PAPER NO 61
LONDON: HOME OFFICE POLICE DEPARTMENT

....

Editor: Barry Webb
Home Office Police Research Group
50 Queen Anne's Gate
London SW1H 9AT

Police Research Group: Crime Detection and Prevention Series

The Home Office Police Research group (PRG) was formed in 1992 to carry out and manage research relevant to the work of the police service. The terms of reference for the Group include the requirement to identify and disseminate good police practice.

The Crime Detection and Prevention Series follows on from the Crime Prevention Unit papers, a series which has been published by the Home Office since 1983. The recognition that effective crime strategies will often involve both crime prevention and crime investigation, however, has led to the scope of this series being broadened. This new series will present research material on both crime prevention and detection in a way which informs policy and practice throughout the service.

A parrellel series of papers on resource management and organisational issues is also published by PRG, as is a periodical on policing research called'Focus'.

ISBN   1-85893-390-0

Foreword

Depriving criminals of the proceeds of their crimes is important in ensuring that a strong message is sent that crime does not pay. Parliament has enabled the police and the courts to carry out this function through the powerful provisions contained in the Drug Trafficking Offences Act 1986 and the Criminal Justice Act 1988. The legislation has recently been strengthened by the provisions contained in the Criminal Justice Act 1993 and the Drug Trafficking Act 1994 which came into force earlier this year.

In this report, the authors suggest that a number of factors have mitigated against the effective use of these provisions in attempting to investigate, seize and confiscate the proceeds of crime. Whilst identifying the difficulties that exist, the report describes how the new legislative provisions will ease the situation in the courts, and makes some practical suggestions about how the police and other agencies involved in the process might improve their procedures in order to make financial investigation and confiscation more effective in future.

I M BURNS
Deputy Under Secretary of State
Home Office
Police Department
May 1995

Acknowledgments

In a short period that we had available, we covered an enormous amount of ground, both geographically and analytically. Our thanks go primarily to officers in the four areas we examined in depth. There are so many of them that to single out individuals is invidious, but we will name the heads of those sections which gave us particular help. In force-alphabetical order, they are: DI Chris Pope and DS Dai Lewis (Dyfed-Powys); D. Supt. Derek O'Connell, DS Frank Butler, and DS Mike Dixon (Merseyside); former D. Supt Tony Woodgate, DS Jamie Chaplin, DC Hugh Cooper, DS Mandy Davis, DS Andy Sladen, and - especially - DS Dave Tuffey, as well as to DC Mick Badcock, who was attached to the Serious Fraud Office (Metropolitan); and DCI James Perry, DS Tony Grantham, and DC John Turner (South-East Regional Crime Squad). (DCI Perry has now rejoined the Metropolitan Police.) We are grateful also to DC Geoff Callan and DC Jed Wilson (City of London); DI Geoff Wall (Derbyshire); and DC Mick Gagg (South Yorkshire Police), for assistance beyond the call of duty; to the Northern Ireland Terrorist Finance Unit and the RUC Anti-Racketeering Unit; and to all those forces who took pains to complete and return our extensive questionnaire. The Australian Federal Police, the Canadian RCMP, the Dutch CRI and Chief Prosecutor Jan Koers, and the FBI, US Attorney's Office, and Asset Forfeiture Division of the US Department of Justice also gave us valuable help on procedures and problems in their countries.

Outside the police, we are grateful to Sue Taylor, Kennedy Talbot, and all their accountant and lawyer colleagues at the CPS Central Confiscation Unit; to Trevor Millington, Colin Jones and to staff from Investigations Division at HM Customs & Excise; to Andrew Mitchell, Barrister-at-law; to Peter Vallance, of the Home Office's international division; and to Gaynor Houghton-Jones and Janice Woolley (Chief and Assistant Clerk) at Old Street Magistrates' Court. There are many others, whose anonymity we have respected.

Though busy, all of the above gave generously of their time and their thoughts, from which we have all benefitted. Finally, our thanks go to Warwick Maynard and colleagues at the Police Research Group, who assisted us through some delicate negotiations and contributed their commentary on our draft work. For the final version, we alone are responsible.

Michael Levi
Lisa Osofsky

The Authors

Michael Levi is Professor of Criminology and Director of the White-Collar and Organised Crime Research Unit at the University of Wales College of Cardiff

Lisa Osofsky was given leave of absence from the US Attorney's Office, Chicago, to work on this study

Executive summary

No one who reviewed the current state of confiscation of the proceeds of crime in England and Wales in any detail would be likely to judge it a success. To summarise, the main difficulties are as follows:

(1)   Relatively few 'Mr Bigs' have been convicted in the courts and consequently, few are available to have their assets confiscated. Indeed, few have been charged, and therefore have not even had their assets frozen.

(2)   The confiscation order cannot 'reclaim' the past 'entertainment' expenditures of proceeds of crime by people - whether drugs traffickers, fraudsters or other offenders - who have no apparent assets. Our interviews and what criminological evidence there is on persistent offenders' lifestyles suggests that - except for cash 'floats' and other assets found directly on them, plus sometimes ostentatiously decorated homes - most medium and low-level offenders 'spend as they go' and have low savings ratios. (Adler, 1993; Dorn et al. 1992; Fagan, 1994; Gold and Levi, 1994; Levi 1981; Maguire, 1982; Shover and Honaker, 1992). In fraud and other property crimes where the offender is not caught very soon after the offence, there are unlikely to be sufficient funds remaining even to compensate victims, let alone to yield any surplus to the Treasury.

(3)   It is only the recent provisions of the Criminal Justice Act 1993 (CJA 1993) which make it easier to come back to the court if assets are discovered subsequent to the making of a confiscation order, and thus may generate greater sums confiscated in the future. Although these assets may in fact be the proceeds of 'new crimes', the offenders may not find it convenient to make this claim.

(4)   There is generally no *organisational* incentive for anyone to deal vigorously with confiscation matters and clearly it is for the police and HM Customs & Excise to motivate staff and juggle conflicting priorities. Any rewards are based around the satisfaction that the police and prosecutors may get (a) from competently completing a challenging job against wily 'opponents'; and/or (b) from causing stress to and - they believe - temporarily incapacitating (usually low-level) traffickers by removing from them their 'working capital'. (There is thus some capacity to argue that restraint and confiscation can produce a more effective result that imprisonment.) Neither at police nor at customs (or subsequent) resource-allocation levels is there any measurable benefit for spending time on seizure and confiscation matters. There are no obvious performance indicators which translate measures of high-level political concern into the working practices of police, prosecutors, and courts. The only possible impact on performance measures within the present framework would be if the financial (as contrasted with penal) incapacitation of individuals subjected to confiscation orders led to a large, visible and attributable diminution in levels of recorded crime in the same geographical areas covered by the unit of investigative/prosecutorial cost. Most of those interviewed in this study agreed that this is unlikely.

(5)   Perhaps because confiscation cases are dispersed among so many counsel and judges, and because the issues are essentially civil in nature and consequently are alien grafts upon the criminal justice system, few people are able to gain any real expertise and many still appear to find the process of deciding on benefit and realisable assets confusing and unattractive. The consensus among those police and lawyers interviewed is that though they take their role seriously, some counsel and Crown Court judges appear to view the rigorous implementation of confiscation procedures as a marginal or even dispensable adjunct to their core tasks of dealing with the case to the point of jury decision and imposing sentence (of which confiscation is not formally part). Consequently, the implementation of the confiscation process is erratic. The imminent publication of consolidated guidance (to police, courts and public) should help in the education process.

(6)   Once an order is imposed, there is little reason for prosecutors or court staff to spend money on enforcing it unless the sums likely to be recovered are estimated obviously (at the time) to exceed the costs of enforcement. Where professional receivers (i.e. accountants) have to be paid, this comes out of the assets received or, where these are insufficient or the defendant is acquitted, from the Crown Prosecution Service (CPS) or Customs 'bottom line'. While the pursuit of those offenders' assets which are less than the costs of receivership may deprive offenders of their unlawfully obtained assets - the key principled objective of the legislation - it provides no net benefit, or even generates a net cost, to the prosecutors (and thus, indirectly, to the taxpayer).

7)   There is no provision in UK law for courts to officially 'write off'
     confiscation orders. In the past there has, however, been no clear
     incentive for magistrates' courts to enforce the orders by collecting the
     maximum amounts ordered to be confiscated, since it has been just as
     easy (in performance indicator terms) to treat funds as irrecoverable as
     to recover them. This is also cheaper, since bailiffs have to be
     employed and administrators' time taken up in enforcing orders against
     unco-operative offenders. (In theory, a smaller grant may be made in
     subsequent years to those courts that have outstanding amounts of
     uncollected assets.)

(8) Until the coming into force of the Criminal Justice Act 1993
     (and even after, in the case of non-drug offenders), the only sanction
     for defendants' non-co-operation in liquidating assets held overseas to
     repay confiscation orders was imprisonment, either in lieu of payment
     or as contempt of court. The extent to which offenders would be
     prepared to suffer an additional prison sentence in lieu of payment may
     have been underestimated by those drafting the early legislation.

(9) There are costs and difficulties involved in assessing realisable
     assets of defendants. The downward trend in the property market since
     1989, and the reluctance of police financial investigators to indicate an
     amount of realisable property that might be lower than the offender's
     benefit from crime (which allows the offender to profit from his crimes)
     mean that some confiscation orders are therefore made in over-
     optimistically large sums, and certificates of inadequacy may have to be
     obtained later, which recognise that there is no prospect of the order
     being satisfied. (HM Customs & Excise avoid this by merely citing a
     figure for benefit from crime, putting pressure on the defendant to cite
     a figure for his assets, to avoid an order for the full alleged benefit.)

Combined, these factors may explain why confiscation orders constitute such
a small proportion of the estimated proceeds of drugs trafficking and other
major crimes, and why, in many instances, the amount recovered from cases
where orders are imposed is so modest.

The report identifies a number of ways forward:

(A) Detectives should inform the Force Financial Investigation Unit (FIU) at an early stage of the investigation and keep them informed.

(B) Crown prosecutors, the police and counsel must all communicate.

(C) Policy makers and legislation drafters must continue to communicate with those responsible for implementing the legislation on a day to day basis.

(D) Consideration should be given to removing Magistrates Courts from the process of enforcement of Confiscation Orders and leaving enforcement to the police service, who would be funded accordingly.

(E) Accurate, uniform statistics are essential to any proper assessment of police work in the area of confiscation.

(F) Documents submitted to the High Court and Crown Courts vary between forces, and should be standardised. This would assist CPS branch prosecutors, CCU lawyers, Judges and Magistrates.

(G) Some force wide training in the area of financial investigations with a focus on confiscation would be desirable.

(H) A high turnover of experienced, competent staff in FIUs is undesirable.

(I) Consideration could be given to allowing a percentage of all assets confiscated being returned to the Units for further use in combatting drugs trafficking.

Contents

List of tables

1. Introduction: the principal issues

Background

'Taking the profit out of crime' has been an important rhetorical *motif* in the English-speaking developed world for the past decade. It also carries with it the unintended potential for making some areas of police investigation financially self-sufficient, though this was never the motivation behind the confiscation legislation. In England and Wales, this started in earnest with the Report of the Hodgson Committee in 1984 and the subsequent enactment of a variety of confiscation provisions in the Drug Trafficking Offences Act 1986, the Criminal Justice Act 1988, the Prevention of Terrorism (Temporary Provisions) Act 1989 and the Criminal Justice (International Co-operation) Act 1990. Difficulties experienced with the judicial implementation of the 'reverse onus' liability rules in drug profit confiscation, along with requirements to comply with the recent European Directive and Council of Europe Convention, have led to the revised confiscation provisions in the Criminal Justice Act 1993. There have been two reports of the Home Office Working Group on Confiscation, but up until now there has been no systematic analysis either of 'good practice' in the conduct of financial investigations **or** of the actual and potential benefits and limitations of confiscation (and forfeiture) as a method of combatting drugs trafficking in particular or organised crime in general. It is these gaps that the research was commissioned to fill, on the assumption that despite the stream of legislative reforms, the system has now bedded down sufficiently to be worth reviewing. Preliminary discussions indicated widespread police concern about the resource costs and yield of financial investigation for these purposes.

The research

By mid 1993, the Home Office and the Association of Chief Police Officers (ACPO) had become increasingly concerned that the difficulties of financial investigation and asset confiscation were hampering the police in their efforts to combat 'organised', and particularly drugs-related, crime. The Home Office Police Research Group therefore commissioned this research, which was designed to comprise two core elements:

- to seek to identify 'good practice' in asset investigation and confiscation;

- to review, at a conceptual and practical level, the impact of confiscation upon offenders and upon the organisation of crime.

The objectives of the project were to establish, as far as possible:

- the impact of asset freezing and confiscation provisions on the organisation of crime;

- those investigative strategies and resource deployments which are most likely and least likely to produce benefits;

- the plausible limits of asset confiscation strategies as an approach to tackling organised crime;

- any changes in the legislative and institutional framework of policing which would improve the monetary and arrest yield of financial investigation.

Using observational and interview methods, as well as examination of case files, the study sought to elucidate any common factors in the success of confiscation orders (e.g. reports by financial institutions about transactions which they thought might be the proceeds of crime at an early stage, early imposition of restraint orders, etc.). Similarly, cases in which there was no Order made or, if an Order was made, there was no successful recovery were examined for commonality of factors (e.g. total defendant non co-operation, assets held overseas). Officers in a variety of operational roles, mainly drugs-related, were interviewed in the Dyfed-Powys, Merseyside and Metropolitan police forces, and in the South-East Regional Crime Squad. A questionnaire survey of all other forces in England and Wales was also conducted and some other forces (including the RUC and the Terrorist Finance Unit of the Northern Ireland Office), Regional Crime Squads, and Customs & Excise Investigations Division visited. Police officers and lawyers from other countries, such as Australia, Canada, the Netherlands, and the US, who had experience in the area of asset confiscation were interviewed. Finally, the study benefitted from many discussions with prosecuting counsel, and with a variety of prosecutors and accountancy staff from the Crown Prosecution Service and Customs & Excise, and with representatives from the Lord Chancellor's Department and the Magistrates' Courts.

2. The extent to which confiscated sums approach estimated proceeds of crime

Current levels of confiscation in the UK

Data collected from police forces and from HM Customs & Excise by the National Criminal Intelligence Service (NCIS) suggest that in the period January 1987 (when confiscation legislation was introduced) to December 1993 a total of £62,173,000 was ordered to be confiscated in England and Wales. However, information from petty sessional divisions suggests that from January 1987 to May 1993, only £14,885,415 was either obtained or written off as a result of offenders serving imprisonment in default. The distribution between these categories is unknown, but prior to changes relating solely to drugs trafficking offences in the CJA 1993, the effect of this imprisonment was that offenders retained their assets, if they existed. Thus, less than a quarter of the amounts ordered to be confiscated were actually taken from offenders. The total value of property restrained in these cases is substantially greater than that ordered to be confiscated, partly because defendants can convince the prosecution and/or the court that the property does not belong to them, partly because it is lawfully diminished by legal and domestic expenses prior to conviction, and partly because the value of property has been incorrectly estimated and/or has declined in the interim. (Several parties noted that heavy legal expenses were a 'no-lose' situation for defendants, since they are betting what would be the government's money on obtaining an acquittal: however, as they acknowledged, it is hard to do anything about this without prejudicing the right to a competent defence.)

In the light of data reliability considerations and developing police expertise, it makes sense to focus on the recent data. In the calendar year 1993, 1,595 drugs trafficking confiscation orders were made in the sum of £11,952,000. In relation to non-drugs offences, some £951,186 was ordered to be confiscated under the Criminal Justice Act 1988, plus an additional £990,000 in one of only two Serious Fraud Office cases to date where confiscation orders have been made. Only nine forces were involved in any confiscation cases under the Criminal Justice Act 1988, and only three were involved in more than one such case. This indicates the very modest impact that confiscation has had upon non-drugs cases, though the cases that do happen tend to attract a great deal of publicity. It is in the non-drugs cases that police dissatisfaction with the confiscation process is greatest. Table 1 gives a breakdown of the sources and types of orders by value.

Table 1: Value of Confiscation Orders made in England and Wales, 1993 (£'000s)		
	Drugs orders	**Non-drugs orders**
Serious Fraud Office	-	990
HM Customs and Excise	7,809	723
Regional Crime Squads	1,130	228
Metropolitan Police	1,607	
Other force	1,406	
TOTALS	11,952	1,941
Source: National Criminal Intelligence Service		

In addition to the complications arising from the fact that the individual police forces collate figures by calendar year (as requested by NCIS), while the Regional Crime Squads and HM Customs & Excise do so by financial year, the use of annual data on confiscation raises problems of interpretation. This is because the sum involved in the confiscation order can appear in several years, making the yield from confiscation orders look lower than it actually is.

Estimating the proceeds of crime

Before examining the confiscation process and its impact in individual cases, it may be helpful to consider how much money might *potentially* be liable to confiscation in the UK. This sum has two components: (i) what is the total income from crime, and (ii) how much of that benefit is likely to become available for confiscation (i.e. is 'realisable benefit' within the terms of the legislation, discussed in section 4). This entails examining the spending and saving habits of offenders, about which comparatively little is known. The UK 'criminal economy' - excluding tax evasion - may be divided into two areas: (1) so-called 'victimless' or 'racketeering' crimes, where the crime is indulged in consensually (such as drugs or prostitution) or where money is extorted without the crime being reported to the police; and (2) property crime for gain, where money or goods are stolen or defrauded. Estimating the amount of money generated by drugs trafficking and other category 1 crimes generally is a particularly hazardous business.

As a first step, it is possible to estimate the losses from property crimes *with* victims (for a more sophisticated analysis of some of these issues, see Levi and Pithouse (forthcoming)). In relation to fraud, as of April 1993, the Serious Fraud Office (1994) dealt with over £6 billion in fraud, and in 1991-92 - the only year for which this has been calculated - the Headquarters Fraud Division of the CPS dealt with £3.9 billion in fraud (Levi, 1993). However, these included the sums at risk rather than solely the amount actually taken; the latter figure is not available from any source.

The proceeds of other forms of property crime recorded in 1992 are summarised in table 2. The amounts stolen net of recoveries is the figure relevant for our purposes, since what is recovered does not need to be confiscated and does not constitute a 'benefit' for the purposes of the legislation.

Table 2: Estimates of the proceeds of property crime, England and Wales, 1992 (£'000s)		
	Gross value stolen	**Value stolen (net of recoveries)**
Domestic burglary	602,361	578,855
Commercial burglary	454,775	414,612
Theft of Motor vehicles	1,728,150	728,280
Other theft	1,234,786	1,190,152
TOTALS	4,020,072	2,913,350
Source: Home Office, Criminal Statistics, England and Wales, 1992.		

There are other proceeds of crime which - in the main - go undetected, unreported, and thus unrecorded. The Association of British Insurers estimated, for example, that £800 million was lost in 1992. Similarly, the British Retail Consortium (1994) study revealed that in 1992, the economic losses to retailers arising out of crime net of recoveries were some £1,400 million, as shown in table 3. These exclude the cost of repairs and collateral costs to businesses, since they do not bring profits to offenders, but include unreported losses, and thus the data are not comparable with those in table 2.

Table 3: Estimates of the proceeds of crime against retailers, Great Britain, 1992 (£'000s)	
Burglary	222,500
Customer theft	471,200
Staff theft	549,200
'Shrinkage' attributed to crime	84,100
Cheque/credit card fraud	21,700
Robberies	24,200
TOTALS	1,372,900
Source: British Retail Consortium, 1994	

On the (high-sided) assumption that all new goods are resold for half of their value, criminals obtained £769 million from the retail sector in 1992. On the generous assumption that offenders resell goods stolen from burglaries and non-vehicle thefts and obtain one third of their value - it is often closer to one tenth - then the value of unrecovered goods shown in table 2 would net them £728 million. The cost of thefts of vehicles has been omitted, because it is unclear how many of them would have been resold. The benefits to those who purchase stolen goods, even though in theory many of them have committed the offence of handling stolen goods and would be liable to conviction and confiscation, have also been omitted. In practice, officers from individual forces and Regional Crime Squads state that convictions of receivers involving more than £10,000 are very rare.

Combining the British Retail Consortium and recorded property crime data, we reach £1,497 million profits from crime other than financial services and bankruptcy frauds. However, in taking account of current legislation, all property crimes in which less than £10,000 was chargeable in one indictment should be excluded, for this is the trigger point for confiscations under the Criminal Justice Act 1988. Fraud excepted, this leaves few property offenders at risk of confiscation. Although one cannot readily merge recorded crime statistics with offender indictment statistics (which are not collated centrally by value of crimes charged), in England and Wales, in 1992, there were 36,264 thefts (almost all of them involving vehicles, most of which are recovered) and 10,465 burglaries recorded as each costing £10,000 or more. **This amounts to a sum of around £460 million profits from property crime open to confiscation in 1992.** Though these data exclude the cost of frauds (other than recorded 'thefts by employees') and of robberies - which are no longer published in the criminal statistics - in practice, these would represent the likely upper limit for confiscations.

It is a matter of speculation how much of that money is saved, rather than being used for current living expenses and for 'treats' to impress friends and neighbours, but there is no evidence that offenders have high savings ratios. Rather, they are likely to be party goers who spend the money as they go along and, though their assessable benefit from crime may be high, little of that may be realisable for confiscation purposes.

Turning now to drug trafficking crime, it is likely that we can regard the customary 'ten per cent assumption' - that customs officers confiscate 10 per cent of all the drugs entering the UK - as being entirely speculative, particularly when it is assumed that this percentage is constant over time and between drug types. Given the bulk weight of cannabis, for example, one would predict that the proportion that is seized would be greater than the proportion of cocaine or refined heroin seized. However if, for example, the quantity of heroin reaching the distribution level of the market was around 8,000 kilos in 1992 - see Sutton and Maynard (1992) for some detailed analysis of the estimation issues - and one multiplies that by the average street price, this generates gross sales figures for heroin to non-dealing users and to dealer-users of an estimated £584.7 million in 1990. Likewise, though the data are not available for other crimes, one could build up a model of total street expenditure on narcotics (ignoring factors such as male and female sex-for-drugs and criminal forms of barter encountered during our research, such as shoplifting and credit cards-for-drugs). Gold and Levi (1994) suggest that the **order of magnitude** estimate here of *cash proceeds* initially deposited for laundering and therefore theoretically available for confiscation could be as low as £100 million per annum, though there is ample scope for debate about this and the true figure is likely to be higher.

To conclude, by any *conservative* reasoned estimate of the proceeds of crime in England and Wales, the sums of money ordered for confiscation, let alone those actually confiscated, appear to be proportionately very low. Part of this has a very simple explanation: confiscation can relate only to the proceeds of convicted drugs trafficking offenders or to those few non-drugs trafficking offenders who are convicted *on a single occasion* of offences whose total *realisable benefit* is greater than £10,000. In the case of crimes that do not obtain cash or negotiable instruments equivalent to cash, the total obtained by the offence would have to be much higher: perhaps £100,000 for a burglar, assuming a 10 per cent return on fenced goods; or somewhat closer to £10,000 to the 'fence' himself, since his profit margin presumably is higher than that of the burglar. A more pragmatic approach would require us to estimate the net proceeds of crime *for those offenders liable to confiscation who are convicted*, but that has not been possible within the confines of this study.

Thus, to summarise, there is more than likely to be as much as £460 million of proceeds from property crimes and £100 million from drugs trafficking crimes available for confiscation per annum. Yet confiscation orders were only made to a total value of £14 million during 1993.

The US and UK systems compared

Despite these difficulties and the low relative level of confiscation we are not proposing the adoption in England of the US approach to forfeiture. However, since much of the impetus 'trailblazing' the confiscation process comes from North America and since many of those interviewed in this study spoke enviously of what they (often inaccurately) imagined happened there, it is worth noting the huge contrast between the scale of asset forfeiture (both civil and criminal) in the US, compared with England. There, the grand total **received** by the US Marshals service was $3,275.8 million over the slightly longer comparable period of January 1985 to September 1993, and was $555.7 million from January to September 1993 alone. In other words, the US Marshals actually obtained £140 for every £1 obtained in England and Wales, and their receipts in 1993 alone were over 20 times the total receipts in England and Wales since 1987. Too much must not be made of these data: variation in levels of GNP, for example, will clearly be an influence outside the confiscation arena. This comparison may be misleading, inasmuch as US enforcement costs are high, totalling $2,229.8 million, leaving a net surplus of 'only' $948.8 million over the whole period and $30 million from January to September 1993. Since there is no full costing of UK confiscation it is difficult to make comparisons, but the *net* figure for 1993 alone in the US is greater than the *gross* total actually obtained in England since 1987. Some other contrasts are instructive. Whereas our survey turned up only about three cases nationally in 1993 where businesses had been 'seized' as part of a confiscation or proposed confiscation case, the US Federal system had 4,499 properties and businesses under seizure in 1993, totalling $859 million by value.

Nevertheless, despite the much larger volumes forfeited in the US (with consequent benefit to the Treasury and to enforcement agencies which benefit directly), scepticism has been expressed regarding the 'supply side' impact of forfeiture on offenders. Karchmer (1985) observes:

> "1981 federal currency and asset seizure and forfeiture actions, as well as narcotics-related Internal Revenue Service civil tax penalties and assessments, totalled $296 million. Comparing the midpoints of other reputable estimates of 1981 narcotics proceeds ($45 billion) with government data on 1981 removal actions (those instituted in 1981 but probably involving income generated in several prior years), one concludes that $0.0062 out of every illegally earned dollar from narcotics traffic is subject to the initiation of some type of government removal action. This figure loses further significance when one looks at the outcomes of various removal actions: less than half the amounts involved in seizure and forfeiture actions were actually surrendered to the government, and no more than 2 per cent of IRS jeopardy and termination assessments (which totalled $81.3 million in 1981) ended up being collected. In the light of these statistics, the value of asset removal strategies is highly questionable."

Action against white-collar offenders and 'corrupt organisations' may have changed the yield - and has certainly enhanced the gross and net sums received - somewhat since that date, but Karchmer's core argument about the modest *ratio* of seizures to proceeds from crime still retains its validity as a critique of the likely overall impact of asset forfeiture on narcotics sales. This is particularly so when we look at the data in the light of the guesstimates of the volumes of money laundered in the US, the UK, and Australia (Senate, 1994) although, at least in relation to cash, Gold and Levi (1994) argue that these amounts are probably greatly overstated.

The US's greater proceeds arise due to a number of factors:

> (i) The much higher focus of their authorities on white-collar crime where there are more assets likely to be found among professionals and others with more fixed assets and less extravagant spending patterns.

(ii)   More emphasis on long-term investigations into organised crime groups and their associated networks.

(iii)   The focus on professionals (lawyers, accountants, brokers) who are adjuncts to traffickers and who are likely to have substantial assets.

(iv)   The existence of the Racketeer Influenced Corrupt Organizations Act 1970 (RICO) and other 'organized crime' provisions which make it easier to extract heavy penalties by civil as well as criminal actions.

(v)   The US authorities' extensive use of civil (in rem) forfeiture powers. These powers enable 'tainted' property to be forfeited without the need for a criminal conviction. In the UK, confiscation can only take place after a criminal conviction for a relevant offence, except for the 'cash across borders' provisions in Part II of the Drug Trafficking Act 1994.

Although the US authorities do take cognisance of the enforcement costs of asset forfeiture in individual cases, the *Federal* system appears to be more consistently committed than ours to the principle of depriving criminals of their assets, irrespective of whether or not this always produced a profit in individual instances. This balance between maximum deprivation and cost-effective enforcement is a policy decision which could be more fully articulated by the UK government than it is. If the UK is to shift further towards maximum deprivation of assets, institutional costs must be fully compensated. In this respect, some police officers complained that the current *perceived* CPS Central Confiscation Unit (CCU) policy of not going for restraint and confiscation below £2,000 (or the varied sums up to £15,000 that they *believed* to be the CCU minimum threshold policy) has prevented them from confiscating the working capital of street-level dealers, which they view as an important objective, irrespective of whether or not it is financially cost-effective to make and enforce the Order. Officers welcome the fact that the new provisions of the Criminal Justice Act 1993 enable them to avoid wasting time making detailed reports to the court on offenders whom they 'know' have no assets, but they expressed concern about a high 'minimum threshold figure' for confiscation applications by the CPS.

However, our interviews with the CCU indicate that there is some misunderstanding of the situation on the part of the police. As discussed elsewhere, the involvement of the CCU is necessary only where assets have to be restrained through the High Court in London, though they are available for consultation on other cases. The CCU are *not* prosecutors of cases. In a drugs trafficking case, there is nothing to stop a CPS local branch prosecutor applying for a confiscation order for any sum, however small. There is no minimum threshold in drugs cases which fall to be dealt with under the Drug Trafficking Offences Act 1986. The CCU will continue to operate a discretionary threshold in cases which fall to be dealt with under the new confiscation regime (introduced by the Drug Trafficking Act 1994). The threshold for non-drugs trafficking cases, is set at £10,000 under the CJA 1988 and is a way of rationing scarce resources to deal with the more complex cases where restraint is seen as 'worthwhile' and as 'cost-effective' given (a) administration costs and (b) allowable (by case law) expenses to defendants, such as legal costs and public school fees for the defendant's children (if the latter are already there). It would be irrational for the CCU to spend public funds in pursuing restraint cases if the offender would not be able to retain the assets anyway, and the English courts are willing (unlike the Dutch courts) to permit the funds to be spent on those purposes. So the main effect of the refusal of the CCU to become involved is to prevent assets from being restrained and receivers from being appointed, not to prevent confiscation altogether.

It could be countered that asset forfeiture US-style has some (unintended) negative consequences. First, it shifts the focus of criminal investigations away from spendthrifts, towards otherwise criminally marginal persons such as professional people, who have assets which can be seized and who are caught by the widely drafted legislation. Second, it can lead to an inappropriate level of zeal and tendency to abuse civil liberties on the part of law enforcement personnel, who - since the confiscation of stylish, high powered transportation for law enforcement officers' use is a benefit to them - develop a *personal* interest in a targeting regime which complements the *institutional* dependence on assets recovered for the survival of (or at least the technical resources made available to) their agency. The selection of targets for forfeiture can sometimes appear capricious and vindictive, though recent appellate decisions have reinforced *offence proportionality* in the forfeiture process.

These negative side-effects appear to be more true of local and state police than of the federal authorities. Countervailing these pressures to maximise yields are the attendant risks that 'realisable benefits' from crime will be *under*stated as a consequence of corruption on the part of law enforcement officers. For the above reasons, any elevation of the status of criminal confiscation is something which should be approached with care, particularly where it entails *core* funding on the basis of results.

3. The principles and impacts of confiscation

Philosophical justifications for confiscation

In England and Wales, the theory underlying confiscation is that it relieves the criminal of financial gain from unacceptable social behaviour. It is not part of the punitive component of the sentence and does not mitigate or aggravate it (Ashworth, 1992; Mitchell et al., 1992). However, those involved in investigating the proceeds of crime view confiscation as an attack that truly hurts the criminal by depriving him of the monetary benefits that he covets most, and undermining his credibility as a criminal. The criminal who convinces his jailmates that 'his' assets are waiting for him when he is released, gains status in the eyes of his fellows; conversely, the one who is publicly stripped of 'his' assets loses status.

Another philosophical justification for confiscation is its possible deterrent value. If criminals are convinced that "crime does not pay," and that (if caught) they will be unable to retain their ill gotten gains, then, presumably, at least some criminals will be deterred from committing certain crimes. Some of our own interviews with offenders would suggest that many view the proceeds of crime as their 'entitlement', and removing this presumed entitlement would naturally cause resentment and be seen as 'punishment'. *Prima facie*, however, there seems no reason to expect that confiscation will lead such individuals to abstain from crime in future - it might simply lead to greater determination to 'get their just deserts' (as they see them) though, as in snakes and ladders, they may find it hard to get back to where they were before. Moreover if, as we and police officers largely agree, many of the proceeds of crime are spent before arrest (and *a fortiori*, before confiscation), the deterrent as well as punitive and reparative effects will be modest. (Customs officers note that middle and high-level traffickers are less spendthrift, and action taken against them might have correspondingly greater economic benefits, though whether others would be deterred thereby remains speculative.)

The impact of confiscation on offenders

It is difficult to measure the impact that confiscation has on offenders and on the 'criminal organisations' - an often problematic phrase, as the police appreciated - with which some offenders associate. Because of the length of their sentences, the more serious offenders would not have had much opportunity to display the effects of confiscation, which anyway would be hard to separate from the possible deterrent effects of lengthy imprisonment. There were, however, many illustrations of the importance with which offenders viewed confiscation: for example, one defendant pleaded guilty at

Winchester Crown Court to 21 out of 24 charges - gaining sentencing credit for avoiding a three month trial - but then fought a confiscation hearing which lasted three weeks. However, the prevailing view among the police is that, while confiscation hurts the criminal by taking from him what he values most, it does little to put him or his organisation out of business. One reason for the general lack of impact of confiscation on individuals and groups is that if the assets of an individual are confiscated, that individual can be replaced in an organisation. When the individual leaves prison, provided that he is 'of good standing' among his fellows, he may return to the organisation and can acquire goods (such as drugs) on credit. Even the individual criminal who is on his own appears (from anecdotal evidence regarding repeat offenders) to need little in the way of assets to return to the life of crime following a jail sentence and asset confiscation. Accordingly, confiscation does not put the individual out of business, though - like individual bankruptcy - it may reduce the scale of his activities in the short and perhaps the longer run. It should be acknowledged that putting individual offenders out of business was never part of the rationale underlying confiscation in the first place. Another perhaps unduly cynical view is that confiscation following Crime A does little more than make the offender more careful with his assets when he commits Crime B. Thus, the offenders appear to get smart about hiding their assets once they have been deprived of them. This is likely to be particularly true of the medium-level offenders, the higher-level ones having planned for confiscation risks just as they plan their money-laundering via corporate nominees.

This pessimistic conclusion about offenders learning not to commit mistakes is not true of all offenders, however. Some may be too stupid to learn the lessons of the past, while others may not have the sophisticated understanding or contacts to deal more subtly with their assets, but may be unwilling to give up crime. Many will continue to do what they appear to do anyway: spend their money as they go along, living a short-term hedonistic (and/or addicted) lifestyle in which savings - and hence confiscation - have little meaning. This does not rule out individual effects. For example, where drugs are supplied to dealers by wholesalers on credit, one possible scenario is that the confiscation of dealers' assets can lead to heavy retribution by the enraged wholesalers. The view of most police officers is that confiscation has had little effect on general levels of offending, even though it may have some modest individual effects.

Overall, they saw confiscation as a disruptive influence, in confiscating medium/low level offenders' working capital, making them trade 'from the bottom' again, with the greater conviction risks attached to street-level dealing. It upsets them considerably, reduces their status in the eyes of fellow offenders, and is one of the few things that can force them to supply information about their activities if they want to avoid confiscation of those assets of which the authorities have knowledge. This unofficial 'plea-bargaining' was viewed by officers as a reasonable tactic to employ during an investigation, but was the source of police concerns about the role played by Crown prosecutors or counsel (see section 6 on relationships with those agencies).

Regarding entire organizations, the cases studied and officers and prosecutors interviewed all expressed similar sentiments. In their confiscation work, they are not targeting whole organisations, nor (with some very few exceptions) the heads of organisations. Thus, their work does not hamper the ability of criminal organisations to conduct their activities. These comments applied even to several Regional Crime Squad cases, though the South-East Regional Crime Squad were seeking to target international money-laundering operations, and their cases under restraint and confiscation reflected this. It can also - though this was rare - be a source of obtaining good informants.

The impact of confiscation on the criminal investigation

This study did not seek to examine whether financial investigation has an impact on criminal investigation. Moreover, it is difficult to determine what would have occurred if an agency other than the police had responsibility for assessing the realisable benefits from crime. It appeared, however, that whilst financial investigation produces little benefit for the core investigation when drug users are dealing merely to sustain their own habit, it does tend to indicate to the court the *scale* of the offender's dealing, possibly indirectly affecting sentencing, by discrediting the offender's claim that this was an isolated offence. Such an effect on perceptions of the offender's deserts is currently not possible in non-drugs cases, for there the realisable benefit is restricted to the offence(s) of conviction. Financial investigations can pinpoint times and places where the suspect was, and thus either corroborate or discredit his statements in the crime under investigation. They can also lead to the discovery of other offences, as when drugs dealers are also involved in fraud. As one officer observed:

> "The evidence gained during the course of financial investigations does indicate to the defence that evidence is available which may establish an undisclosed income or an income or expenditure the defendant might find very difficult to justify. It also establishes

involvement in other crimes such as fraud involving the Department of Social Security. The result is that the defendant is persuaded that a trial would ultimately be futile. Almost every case could benefit from a financial investigation particularly in the case of drugs. Very few people when making money at any level can avoid the temptation to spend it. Once spent it almost always becomes identifiable no matter how small. It is often the case that defendants hide information relating to their income but are more than willing to tell you their expenditure. This is because they believe that if they have large commitments and only a small stated income they will protect themselves. In fact this works to the contrary. An expenditure above that of income clearly indicates another source of income and it is often here that small time drug dealers or criminals fall down."

Other circumstances where financial investigations *were* useful include:

- Proving that the majority of credits to a bank account were housing benefit cheques issued to registered drug addicts.

- Unearthing significant evidence showing that the subject had purchased equipment which had been used on a high value burglary.

- Showing that between the date of offence and arrest, the offender spent the equivalent of one third of the proceeds of the armed robbery over and above his legitimate income.

- Ascertaining that large amounts of money had been deposited in a bank account which had originated from drug trafficking. The offender was arrested and charged with supplying. He asserted that the funds had been accrued as a result of car dealing. Financial investigations rebutted this and the Court agreed with the Section 3 Statement.

- Establishing the motive for the offence in a murder enquiry.

- Establishing income in excess of means, which was appropriate to the goods stolen in an enquiry into professional car theft.

- Following the execution of a search warrant, an unemployed man was arrested and charged with possessing drugs with intent to supply others. The amount of drugs recovered was small and alone would perhaps not have substantiated the charges. Examinations of the defendant's financial background evidenced monies paid into his bank account which could not be ascribed to lawful income and which he could not/would not explain. He was convicted of the trafficking offences and a confiscation order was made.

- Four persons were arrested in possession of 10 kilos of cannabis. It was anticipated that the quantity of drugs would be much greater and books found at the premises tended to indicate this. The defendants each denied responsibility for the drugs, blaming the other. There was other evidence directed towards two of the individuals but limited evidence of association and limited evidence to connect the deal books with either of them. Examination of the deal books showed a minimum of £480,000 worth of deals. The financial investigation and the resultant analysis was able to link both individuals with the books and to identify one of the individuals as the supplier and the man receiving the majority of the cash from the sale of the drugs. Through analysis of home and mobile telephones, compared with entries in the deal books, police were able to establish direct links between both persons and identify those persons appearing as purchasers linking them to both suspects. This was essential to the case.

- A defendant was arrested and charged with the possession of drugs with intent to supply. The defendant was employed in charge of an incinerator used for the disposal of drugs by HM Customs and Excise. He had developed a method of avoiding incineration and was removing the drugs, which were eventually re-sold. Although he was only charged with the removal of one consignment it was suspected that he had been responsible for the removal of consignments over a period up to six years. The defendant made no admissions regarding past involvement and did not involve any other person. Financial investigation into the defendant and his family clearly identified the involvement of his brothers and his father. Investigations into the movement of monies were essential in obtaining evidence against these persons for both supplying drugs and laundering the proceeds. The investigation identified the times at which influx of the money took place, and these coincided with consignments of drugs to the incinerator.

- A case against a dealer involving a very complex investigation including 'underground banking' resulted in the identification of benefit in excess of £600,000 and a confiscation order of £43,000. During his trial, certain statements made to the court by defence counsel were able to be refuted as a result of information obtained and by reference to certain of the documents recovered during the financial investigation into the case.

- Following the arrest of a known drug dealer, a relatively small amount of cannabis resin was recovered from his home address which this man stated was only intended for his own use and that of his close friends and associates. However, the subsequent analysis of two encoded notebooks identified benefit in excess of £75,000. When the section 3 statement was served on the defendant he immediately contacted the police, through his solicitor, and was interviewed further regarding his finances. During the interview, in addition to clarifying the extent to which he had benefitted from his activities, the defendant also implicated further persons whom he had previously refused to name. When he appeared before the Crown Court he pleaded guilty and was convicted as a "commercial" rather than a "social" dealer.

The above cases illustrate the benefits that *can* arise for criminal investigation generally from the appropriate use of financial intelligence. The effectiveness of the legislation in enabling the courts to restrain and to confiscate the assets of convicted offenders plainly depends upon the efficiency of those whose task it is to bring those assets to light and upon the legal possibilities of following the money trail.

4. Restraint and confiscation legislation: a summary

The vast majority of confiscation cases arise in the area of drugs trafficking. Whatever the current controversies over what is the most rational strategy for dealing with drugs users, perhaps more than any other crime facing society today, the drug problem has captured the attention of the public, the media, and the law enforcement community. Confiscation is widely advocated as an important part of the Crown's arsenal of weapons used to combat the drugs problem. It is not surprising, then, that the law on confiscation has developed largely in the area of drugs trafficking. Since one of our conclusions is that a 'significant number' of those entrusted with implementing the legislation - both in the courts and after orders have been made - have only modest awareness of its provisions, this section contains a detailed review of the legislation and how it is supposed to work. Later sections go on to discuss how it works in practice. (For more detailed and legally annotated reviews, see Mitchell *et al.*, 1992; Levi and Osofsky, 1994; and Thomas, 1982, 1994.)

The development of confiscation legislation in England and Wales

As a reaction to the impotence of the courts in forfeiting any more than the property used in the actual commission of the crime(s) of conviction, the Drug Trafficking Offences Act (DTOA) was enacted in 1986. The Act embodied legislation aimed at identifying the proceeds of crime and freezing and confiscating them. About two years later, Parliament enacted laws permitting confiscation following convictions for crimes other than drugs trafficking. Confiscation under the Criminal Justice Act (CJA) 1988 is limited strictly to indictable offences and certain summary offences where the defendant has benefitted by more than £10,000 **and** where his assets can be shown to exceed that figure.

These two statutes are the primary avenues through which confiscation of the proceeds of crime may be effected in England. In 1995, amendments to these Acts have come into force in the new Criminal Justice Act 1993 (CJA 1993). The discussion that follows takes into consideration all relevant changes in the law of confiscation as the result of the new Act.

Restraint and charging orders

While they relate to criminal proceedings, restraint and charging orders are actually civil in nature, and there was widespread agreement among those we interviewed that this mixture of the civil and the criminal generated difficulties for the police and for some prosecutors in dealing with unfamiliar processes. The purpose of both types of orders is to prevent the dissipation or depreciation of assets which may be confiscated from a convicted criminal. Restraint and charging orders, however, may be issued long before criminal conviction. Under the DTOA and the CJA 1988, the High Court may issue restraint and charging orders as soon as a defendant is arrested for a crime covered by the confiscation laws, or even earlier when the Crown is able to establish that a charge will be forthcoming within a reasonable time. Broadly speaking, these orders serve to hold in abeyance all dealings with certain assets in which the defendant holds an interest pending resolution of the criminal charges against him. Once issued, restraint orders may remain in effect until the defendant is acquitted or a confiscation order is made and satisfied.

Restraint orders are made against specified persons and prevent the restrained parties from dealing in any way with all assets that may be necessary to satisfy a confiscation order. As a practical matter, restraint orders typically list any financial institutions and account numbers, vehicle descriptions and registration numbers, details of real property, stock, and unit trusts in which the defendant *is known or believed to hold* an interest, though there may be other assets unknown to the authorities. All parties with notice of the order, including bankers, financial brokers, and solicitors are subject to its proscriptions.

The confiscation order, which will not be entered until after conviction, may not exceed the defendant's benefit from crime or the value of his assets, whichever is less. Under the CJA 1988, benefit is limited to that derived from the crimes of conviction and crimes formally 'taken into consideration' by the court at that time. In contrast, under the DTOA benefit includes all payments and rewards acquired by the defendant throughout his purported history as a drug dealer regardless of the specific charges of which he has been convicted. The amount that may be restrained is limited on the same principles. In practice, however, since restraint orders are often obtained early on in criminal proceedings, before detailed analysis of the defendant's benefit and realisable property is possible, they are frequently couched in broad terms to try to ensure ultimate satisfaction of the confiscation order.

Restraint orders apply not only to assets in a specified person's control or possession at the time that the order is made, but also to property transferred to that person after the making of the order. In addition, restraint and charging orders may cover gifts made either directly or indirectly by the defendant. The time frames for catching gifts made by the defendant vary under the two Acts. Under the DTOA all gifts made "since the beginning of the period of six years ending when the proceedings were instituted against him" may be the subject of an order of restraint. Under the CJA, only gifts "made by the defendant at any time after the commission of the offence" may be included in a restraint order. This latter issue can reduce the 'yield' from confiscation, since for court presentational reasons, charges in fraud or corruption or living on immoral earnings cases may be focused within a very limited time frame and CJA cases tie the sums confiscated to the charges proven.

Restraint orders may apply to property that is located outside the jurisdiction of the High Court. While worldwide notice of and compliance with such orders is not contemplated by the Acts (for example, the orders have no effect on financial institutions located in foreign jurisdictions) a defendant or restrained person within the jurisdiction may be liable for contempt if he deals with property located beyond its borders. In addition, various treaties and other agreements with foreign authorities provide avenues for mutual cooperation in the early restraint or freezing of assets located outside of the court's jurisdictional boundaries. Alternatively, the High Court may order the defendant to repatriate, or transfer, property to within its jurisdiction so that the full strength of the restraint order may be felt. The sanction for refusal is imprisonment for contempt of court.

To ensure that the existence of all property which should be considered for purposes of restraint is, in fact, made known to the relevant parties, the High Court is empowered to order the defendant to present an affidavit to the prosecution which details all of his realisable property. The disclosure of the information contained in this affidavit cannot be used as evidence against the defendant in the current, or in any other, prosecution, though defendants are likely to feel that this may give the police valuable leads to their associates, in addition to helping police or customs recover what defendants regard as 'their' money.

In contrast to a restraint order, a charging order applies to interests in specified property. This property may include any beneficial interest that the defendant owns in land, securities, such as government or other stock, and units of any unit trust, if such property is affiliated (as described in the Acts) with England or Wales. A charging order is especially well-suited to a situation in which the defendant owns a portion of an asset in which there are multiple interests. The charging order secures the Crown's potential interest in the property and will be discharged when "the [ ] payment [ ] which is secured by the charge is paid into court."

To obtain restraint or charging orders, a prosecutor files an *ex parte* application in the chambers of a High Court judge. As the practice has evolved, all such applications made by the CPS are submitted and reviewed in London, where assigned business is dealt with. The application consists of an originating motion and a supporting affidavit which sets forth the grounds for believing that the defendant has benefitted from a crime to which the confiscation laws apply and, further, details the realisable property sought and the persons holding such property. The affidavit is permitted to contain hearsay and, typically, is made by the investigating financial officer, police or customs.

Once issued, notice and service of the order is the responsibility of the prosecutor, not the police, though in the case of customs, the case officer remains responsible for *personal* service on persons and for informing institutions. The defendant and all other persons restrained by the order must be served. Since the defendant is particularly well-suited to know who is affected by the order, he can be compelled (at least in principle) to identify where those persons can be found so that the prosecutor can provide them with proper notice.

Restraint orders obtained under either the DTOA or the CJA can be varied or discharged by the High Court. Variations may be sought by any person affected by the order and, if agreed between the parties, do not require a hearing in chambers before the High Court. Common reasons for varying restraint orders include allowing the defendant funds to cover 'reasonable' legal fees or permitting him additional living expenses. This is the source of complaints from many police, who observe that the 'benefit from crime' is often dissipated in this process, and that either defence lawyers or defendants' families end up taking monies that 'should' go to central funds. Although defendants are entitled to maintain their innocence, some lawyers and police among those interviewed questioned the appropriateness of allowing the children of defendants to continue to be educated at public school with monies that after their conviction are proven to be proceeds of crime, and voiced the suspicion that funds extracted for legal expenses are sometimes 'kicked back' to clients. If they think that legal costs are unreasonable, Customs & Excise insist that legal expenses are taxed (i.e. formally adjudicated by Court staff) before payment. Where a case is expected to take a long time to come to trial, the defendant is not legally aided and/or where domestic expenses allowed by the court are high, restraint orders are unlikely to be applied for, particularly in CJA 1988 cases where, to trigger a confiscation hearing, there must be more than £10,000 realisable benefit *at the time of the confiscation hearing*. A restraint order may be discharged when the proceedings against the defendant are concluded. The Acts provide that proceedings are concluded "when (disregarding any power of a court to grant leave to appeal out of time) there is no further possibility of a confiscation order being made in the proceedings; or on the satisfaction of a confiscation order made in the proceedings (whether by payment of the amount due under the order or by the defendant serving imprisonment in default)."

Once a restraint order has been issued, the Acts vest in the High Court the power to appoint a receiver "to take possession of any realisable property, and in accordance with the court's direction, to manage or otherwise deal with any property . . . ." Application for appointment of a receiver under these sections may be made only by a prosecutor, and the prosecutor generally pays the costs of the receiver. If the receiver is appointed after the confiscation order is made, the costs are paid - as in ordinary receiverships - from the assets recovered. However, if the receiver is appointed before the order is made - for example, to administer frozen assets - the costs are paid by the CPS. Charges to the department which are not recoverable from assets are avoided wherever possible by both CPS and Customs & Excise.

Appointment of a receiver is particularly appropriate in situations in which property, such as a business or financial firm, must be administered, though in police cases, this happens rarely. Efficient management of such property is necessary to ensure that assets sufficient to satisfy any confiscation order exist when the criminal charges are resolved. As the research demonstrates, there are very few cases in England and Wales in which businesses have to be administered in this way, but disputes with third parties who lay claim to particular assets alleged to be owned (or to be beneficially owned) by the offender are time consuming. A further advantage of receivership is that the receiver can deal directly with the assets, rather than doing so via requests to defendants. Complex issues are generally dealt with by receivers (i.e. professional accountants), provided that there are sufficient assets to repay any estimated professional fees. Customs & Excise appoint receivers more readily than do the CPS, because CPS cases are typically more modest as well as to reduce the risk that they will incur net costs.

Post-conviction confiscation orders

Once a defendant has been convicted of a crime that falls within the confiscation scheme set forth in either the DTOA or the CJA, the court may determine whether confiscation is appropriate. As noted above, the amount of the confiscation order will be capped at the benefit that the defendant has obtained from his criminal activity, or the value of the defendant's realisable property, whichever amount is less.

Prior to the provisions of the Criminal Justice Act 1993 coming into force on 3 February 1995, the Crown Court issued confiscation orders after conviction but before imposing sentence, which imposed great time pressure on police, lawyers, and judges. Now the Crown Court may postpone its determination of confiscation-related issues but pronounce sentence without delay. More than one postponement is permissible as long as confiscation proceedings are concluded within six months of conviction, unless there are exceptional circumstances. In law, confiscation orders take precedence over fines, forfeiture orders and deprivation orders. This is sometimes to the frustration of the police who otherwise might be awarded assets by the court, if forfeiture takes place under the Misuse of Drugs Act.

While both the DTOA and the CJA outline the same basic approach to confiscation, the Acts differ in a number of respects, all of which are particularly relevant to any discussion of the process by which post-conviction confiscation orders are made. First, under Section 1 of the DTOA, if a confiscation hearing is held, and the court finds that the defendant has benefitted from drug trafficking and has realisable assets, the court **must** order confiscation. As amended by the CJA 1993, the court **must** hold a confiscation hearing pursuant to DTOA Section 1 if the prosecutor asks the court to do so and **may** hold a hearing even in the absence of a request by the prosecutor. It is hard to see how realistically the police could by-pass their counsel and communicate to the judge their view that a hearing would be appropriate. Under the CJA 1988, in contrast, the issue of confiscation does not even arise unless the prosecutor has notified the court that a confiscation order of at least £10,000 would be appropriate. Even after this notification, it is entirely within the discretion of the court to determine whether a confiscation order should be issued. A second difference between the two Acts is that, while the CJA 1988 requires a minimum threshold of £10,000 in benefit and realisable property before confiscation will even be considered, under the DTOA, the court must assess the benefit and realisable property regardless of its value. Third, "benefit" under the DTOA is determined by all of the defendant's (adjudicated) drug trafficking activity, whether or not it has resulted in convictions, while the CJA sets benefit at a figure derived solely from the crimes of which the defendant stands convicted, i.e. even if greater assets are found which the defendant cannot explain away by legitimate activity, they cannot be confiscated, once the sums ordered are paid.

The procedure for assessing benefit has been the subject of widespread civil libertarian concern. The sentencing court will assess the defendant's benefit under the DTOA as the combined value of any drug trafficking payments or other rewards received by the defendant at any time. Payments and other rewards are not defined as the net profit the defendant has obtained from drug trafficking but, rather, they are defined as his gross receipts, in money or kind.

The CJA 1993 makes it clear that the standard of proof required to determine whether a person has benefitted from drug trafficking or an offence caught by Part VI of the CJA 1988, and the amount to be recovered, is that applicable in civil proceedings, namely the balance of probabilities. The CJA 1993 makes this clear on the face of the legislation because a number of courts have in the past applied the criminal standard of proof to confiscation hearings (ie beyond reasonable doubt).

In determining the amount of the defendant's benefit, under the DTOA (as amended by the CJA 1993), barring unusual circumstances, the court is *required* to assume the following:

> "(a) that any property appearing to the court:
>   (i) to have been held by him at any time since his conviction, or
>   (ii) transferred to him at any time since the beginning of the period of six years ending when the proceedings were instituted against him was received by him ... as a payment or reward [for trafficking in drugs],
> (b) that any expenditure of his since the beginning of that period was met out of [the proceeds of drug trafficking],
> (c) that, for the purpose of valuing any property received or assumed to have been received by him at any time as such a reward, he received the property free of any other interests in it."

The unusual circumstances that would prohibit application of the required assumptions are either that the assumptions are incorrect in the defendant's case or that their application would result in a serious risk of injustice. Where the court does not apply one or more of the required assumptions, it must state its reasons.

On 9 February 1995 the European Court of Human Rights found that there had been a violation by the United Kingdom of Article 7 of the European Convention on Human Rights, which prohibits the imposition of a heavier criminal penalty than the one which was available at the time the criminal offence was committed. The complainant Peter Welch had a confiscation order imposed on him in 1988 under the Drug Trafficking Offences Act 1986 following conviction, also in 1988, of offences committed before the 1986

Act came into force on 12 January 1987. The Court found, contrary to the government's view, that the confiscation order was a penalty in the particular circumstances of Welch's case and therefore that there had been a violation of Article 7.

In contrast to the DTOA, no assumptions apply when assessing the defendant's benefit under the CJA 1988. Rather, under the CJA, the sentencing court will enter an order where the Crown has established that the convicted defendant:

> "has benefitted from that offence or from that offence taken with some other offence of which he is convicted in the same proceedings, or which the Court takes into consideration in determining his sentence and . . . his benefit is at least [£10,000]."

The size of the defendant's benefit is based on the value of the property that the defendant acquires "as a result of or in connection with the commission" of the offence of which he stands convicted. The amount of equity that a defendant may hold in property acquired through the offence of conviction is irrelevant. Rather, to determine benefit under the CJA, the court asks two simple questions: "what property did [the defendant] obtain as a result of or in connection with the commission of the offence and what was its value?" The proof of connection between the assets held by the defendant or his associates and the offence of conviction is often a matter of dispute, and accounts for part of the disenchantment of investigators and prosecutors with what they term 'crime confiscation'. This is so particularly when 'plea bargains' reduce the amounts involved in the charges, sometimes allegedly without consideration by prosecuting counsel of the confiscation implications of the reduced charges. In non-drugs cases, for example, the reduction after charge-bargaining of benefit to below £10,000 would automatically rule out the possibility of confiscation, though compensation and fines - albeit without criminal restraint orders - remain possible. Considerable concern was expressed that where large numbers of low-value goods were involved - for example, pornography and product counterfeiting - it was unrealistic to press the huge number of charges that would be required to get the sum up to £10,000. This matter is one of a number addressed in Sir John Hannam's Proceeds of Crime Bill, a Private Member's Bill which is currently progressing through Parliament with the Government's strong support.

Once the court has assessed the defendant's benefit, both the DTOA and the CJA require the court to determine whether the defendant can pay the benefit amount. To do so, the court must determine the existence and value of those assets that the defendant may use to satisfy a confiscation order.

Where these assets involve more than simple cash or other liquid assets, valuations are normally required. This is supposed to be the responsibility of the defendant but in practice, the police will often arrange a valuation, which the defendant can then dispute. It was claimed by some interviewees that police valuations tended to be on the high side, possibly because they were often obtained as a favour from professionals to avoid the bureaucratic difficulties of paying for a professional valuation, but also to ensure that defendants did not get away with what the police considered to be 'unjust enrichment'. Once the benefit and realisable asset figures have been determined, the court will order confiscation in the lesser amount. Compensation to victims can be paid out of the amount confiscated, though this creates administrative difficulties. Indeed, for some years, prosecutors avoided applying for confiscation orders where there were victims, though (unknown to many police we interviewed) this policy has now changed. This is important because if prosecutors do not pursue restraint orders rapidly, those offenders whose victims are too poor or risk-averse to make the cross-undertakings for damages and legal expenses in the (civil) court required for the granting of Mareva 'asset-freezing' injunctions will be able to transfer assets outside the jurisdiction. Consequently, any compensation order awarded by the court may be largely academic, because it is not enforceable, and there are no lengthy prison sentences in lieu of non-payment of compensation, as there are for confiscation orders.

As a practical matter, the amount of the confiscation order entered pursuant to either Act is computed as follows. The prosecutor tenders an affidavit sworn by the investigating financial officer - police or customs - indicating his assessment of the amount of benefit and realisable assets in the defendant's possession. There is, in fact, a distinction (and structural tension) between the prosecutor's 'realistic' assessment and the police's much higher one, which is discussed later in the section on enforcement of confiscation orders. While the legislation requires the prosecutor to state only a benefit figure, in CPS - though not in customs - cases, the prosecutor usually details a realisable assets figure as well (because the courts prefer it). It is then up to the defendant to contest any aspect of the prosecutor's statement. If he chooses not to do so, he faces the risk that the Crown Court will accept the prosecutor's statement as accurate and enter a confiscation order in the amount described therein.

In practice, it is the prosecutor who discloses a realisable assets figure (based on a financial investigation) which is usually far less than the benefits figure, either because some assets cannot be found or because it is believed that the offender has spent the money: obviously, the offender who sees his realisable assets understated is unlikely to point this out! Customs & Excise avoid stating a *realisable* benefit figure precisely to keep the defendant uncertain about how many of his/her assets they are aware. In that way, it is hoped that s/he will disclose more than they would otherwise do. We did not have the opportunity to examine how effective this tactic was.

At the time that the confiscation order is issued, the court also fixes a term of imprisonment which the defendant must serve in case of default. That term is determined by statute and the size of the confiscation order dictates the length of the term. Under the new Criminal Justice Act 1993, where a drugs trafficker serves a term of imprisonment in default of payment of a confiscation order, his debt is not expunged, and he remains liable to pay it. There is no similar provision regarding other offences committed under the CJA, so (subject to any civil actions against them) fraudsters and robbers willing to do extra time can continue to go out to 'their' money. Both police and prosecutors questioned the logic behind this legislative distinction, though its practical effect is mitigated by the fact that, currently, CJA proceedings are so rare. This is a matter which is addressed in Sir John Hannam's Proceeds of Crime Bill, which aims to make them more common and financially productive.

Once the Crown Court sets the amount of the confiscation order, the defendant is faced with a choice. Since confiscation orders operate *in personam* (on the individual) rather than *in rem* (on the actual property), nothing in the order dictates what property must be used to satisfy the order. Instead, it is up to the defendant to make this determination. In one case that we looked at, an offender had spent some time on remand, and was released almost immediately following his conviction, but faced the sale of his home to satisfy the confiscation order. He went straight back to drug dealing, presumably to avoid the loss of his home! Clearly, there is every possibility that he would have gone back to dealing anyway, but this is certainly a paradoxical result of confiscation. In other cases, the police are required to return monies and property that they have seized to the defendant to enable him to satisfy the order, but in a number of cases this has resulted in his disappearing with the funds. Examples of other relevant cases are set out in the appendices.

Enforcing confiscation orders

The magistrates' courts normally enforce confiscation orders. However, if the prosecutor applies and the High Court grants the application, a confiscation order may be enforced by a receiver appointed by the High Court. If the defendant has not satisfied the confiscation order during the time-to-pay outlined in it or when his original prison term has expired or is about to expire, and no receiver has been appointed, then the enforcing magistrates' court is faced with a decision. The enforcing court must determine whether to attempt to make the defendant pay or to issue a warrant of commitment to make the defendant serve his sentence of imprisonment in default. The relevant legislation is designed to ensure that the magistrates' courts consider or try all measures to enforce payment before issuing a warrant of commitment. Existing case law has highlighted the need to obtain payment from the defendant rather than simply sending him to jail for an additional term of imprisonment. Magistrates' courts not uncommonly find that the realisable value of, for example, jewellery, is much less than was estimated when the order was made, but unless the order is varied, the offender is still liable to pay. This is a consequence of *in personam* confiscation: many police said that they would prefer to see an order to confiscate particular property, possibly alongside *in personam* confiscation. Such a move may be counter-productive since an advantage of UK confiscation law being value based, is that prosecutors do not have to prove a link between the proceeds of a particular crime and money in a bank account or an item of property before that money or item of property is realised in satisfaction of a confiscation order.

At a minimum, before issuing a warrant of commitment, magistrates' courts are required to inquire, on at least one occasion subsequent to the conviction of the defendant, whether he can satisfy the order. Since, before issuing the confiscation order, the Crown Court will have recently concluded that the defendant does have the means to pay, it seems likely that at least some assets sufficient to satisfy the order would be available. Indeed, as many police and some offenders who were interviewed suggest, it is more plausible that the defendant, after spending some time in jail, might prefer to continue his term of imprisonment rather than be deprived of his criminal proceeds: in non-drugs trafficking, cases, the defendant still has the choice to 'do more bird' and retain his 'loot'.

5. The organisation of financial investigation within the police service

The level of resources devoted: the national picture

All UK forces were sent a questionnaire which asked for information about the level of resources devoted to financial investigation, and problems arising; 35 forces responded.

Half the police forces responding had two officers or fewer in their financial investigation unit (FIU); four had five or more officers. Only five forces had one civilian employed full-time on asset confiscation duties in their FIUs, and two thirds did not have any.

Only 20% of the forces' FIUs spent as much as half of their time on restraint and confiscation duties. The remaining time was spent on following up suspicious transaction reports from financial institutions, general surveillance and developmental intelligence work, and as a 'reserve' for operational detectives arresting serious offenders, particularly in drugs and fraud cases.

80% of forces kept statistics on restraint cases. There was substantial variation in the number of restraint orders handled by each force, but there was no obvious geographical pattern. The most common number of restraint cases dealt with during 1992 and 1993 by FIUs was within the range 1-3 (43% of respondents), followed by 4-6 (14%). Three forces dealt with no restraint cases, and a further three dealt with more than 21 restraint cases. Altogether, slightly under a quarter of forces dealt with four or more restraint cases per year. As for the freezing of businesses - normally an indicator of the use of firms for money-laundering, itself a measure of sophistication (Gold and Levi, 1994) - one force was involved in the restraint of business assets in 1992, and four in 1993. The forces were not all metropolitan ones: they were Derbyshire, Dorset, Durham, Greater Manchester and South Wales. Two thirds of forces used restraint orders in drugs cases; fewer than 10% in fraud and corruption cases; and one force in a burglary case. The remainder were unspecified.

In confiscation cases, figures were less likely to be accurate for the whole period, since many forces did not keep full data before 1993. Moreover, it is dangerous to take raw numbers as a measure of output, since cases may vary enormously in their size and complexity, and a focus on numbers may divert attention towards easy cases at the expense of those which have greater impact (including, though not restricted to, financial recoveries). Nevertheless, eight forces were involved in 50 or more confiscation cases, but eight (plus four Regional Crime Squads) completed fewer than 10 cases in 1993. Almost all of these were for drugs cases: among our respondents there were only 17 Criminal Justice Act 1988 confiscation cases in the whole of England and Wales, almost all of them corruption cases. Table 4 displays the activities of force FIUs, and reflects the predominance of investigations involving street-level rather than wholesaler dealers.

Table 4: Sizes of case dealt with by force FIUs, 1993

Total value of assets traced	No of cases
Under £1,000	662
£1,000 - 2,999	112
£3,000 - 4,999	55
£5,000 and over	86
Total	915

It is the mandate of the five Regional Crime Squads to target and build up cases against major offenders, especially those who cross force boundaries. Table 5 reflects the level of their activity.

Table 5: The work of Regional Crime Squad FIUs

	1991-2	1992-3	1993-4
N of individuals arrested and assets traced	210	247	199
N of restraint and charging orders	101	247	199
N of receivers appointed to deal with assets	3	4	2
Total value of assets traced	£7.5m	£7.5m	£17.6m
Total value of assets ordered confiscated	£2.2m	£2.5m	£1.3m
Value of assets confiscated per officer	£222	£287	£938

The discrepancy in the above table between assets traced and assets confiscated is not just a reflection of acquittals, but arises mainly from the fact that many cases in which assets were traced have not yet resulted in court disposal, as well as the attrition that arises from the assertion of third party ownership claims. This is particularly relevant for the 1993-94 financial year because of the marked increase in the volume of assets traced in enquiries.

The above summary illustrates that practical application of confiscation legislation has varied. Throughout the country, then, there are police financial investigations units (FIUs) responsible for conducting financial investigations, including asset tracing. These are normally headed by detective sergeants or constables; any civilian employees with financial or administrative skills are normally integrated into the FIUs. Depending on the area, the FIU may be attached to a drugs or to a fraud squad. However, most of the confiscation work centres on drugs trafficking offences. The reason some financial investigators remain attached to Fraud Squads is that they are also engaged on fraud work. Our observations and interviews indicate that to maximise the usage of FIUs by drugs squads, close liaison is vital. In practice, success may boil down to personal relations and the 'street cred' of FIU officers with operational detectives.

The development of police expertise in financial investigations

The FIUs which were focused on in detail came into existence between 1989 (in the Metropolitan Police) and 1993, when Dyfed-Powys and the City of London Police created their first Confiscation Units and assigned a detective sergeant and a detective constable respectively to those units full-time. In 1994, Dyfed-Powys employed an analyst - shared with the Fraud Squad - to assist in accountancy and IT needs. Visual presentation via well-designed slides and flow charts were regarded as essential in court, though they created an expectation among counsel that such aids would always be provided. These enhanced expectations of presentation were almost universal among those forces we looked at.

The types of cases worked by the drugs squads seldom lend themselves to a great deal of advance preparation (i.e. financial investigation before arrest), due to the type of target being looked at, and to time and resource constraints. The quantities of drugs seized rarely exceed one kilo. If larger quantities are involved, then the Regional Crime Squad or Customs usually takes the case. The drugs investigations examined generally had around a three-week lifespan. These cases are generally informant-led, and limited resources devoted to them. Thus, while one case involved setting up cameras and microphones to monitor drug dealers who transacted business with an undercover seller (who was working with the police), this scenario was unusual. Even in this case, the investigation was permitted to extend to only four weeks. In the course of investigating one defendant, FIUs often obtain intelligence information on subjects peripheral to the investigation underway which cannot be acted upon without arousing their suspicions. Such information is, however, useful in building up a picture of scale, and maybe connections between people which are denied by them in interview or in court. Most drugs squads have systems in place for filing intelligence for future use, so that FIUs are confident that the majority of their intelligence-gathering efforts do not go to waste.

Generally, the force FIUs (as contrasted with RCS ones) become involved in cases requiring financial investigation where confiscation and/or forfeiture orders are contemplated. They may become involved as early as the preliminary investigation stage or as late as a few hours before a confiscation hearing is scheduled. With exceptions that will be discussed below, the FIUs studied were generally brought into cases *after* arrest, though all of the FIUs expressed a preference for being alerted to the development of cases with financial components as early as possible. While the FIUs believed it was helpful to be introduced to a case early, operational detectives stated that it did not necessarily assist them in their work to bring in the FIUs during the early phases of a case.

A common theme of disaffection among force FIUs was that they would sometimes be informed as late as the day before the case was due to be heard. This makes it impossible to do a thorough job in a more difficult case, though our experience was that without undertaking an enormous amount of further investigation, most defendants probably had few ascertainable assets other than the cash found upon their person, their (normally modest) car, and whatever luxury goods they had at home when it was searched. This modesty of assets may itself be a consequence of confiscation legislation. Limited interviews with offenders and lawyers in the UK and US suggest that some consciously avoid ownership of expensive vehicles - at least within the 'realistic' jurisdiction - to avoid losing them if convicted. Consequently, unsatisfying and disruptive though it may be for the FIU to carry out shoddy work to tight deadlines outside their control, this may not actually be as inefficient as it appears.

The FIUs generally investigate the existence and extent of assets in which targeted individuals or defendants are believed to have an interest. This study reveals that this work usually consists of obtaining bank and building society records (often through use of DTOA Section 27 production orders), land registry, mortgage, and other documents revealing an interest in real property, records related to vehicle purchase and ownership, and documents relating to property such as jewellery and household items. Some FIUs rely upon any account details they find when the offender and his home are searched; others proactively approach as many financial institutions as they find feasible for information about accounts held by the defendant(s) in any names used by them of which they have knowledge. Accounts held in false names and/or in institutions not circulated remain untouched unless the defendant volunteers the information. With some surprising exceptions, FIUs generally receive all of the National Criminal Intelligence Service (NCIS) disclosures for their particular area, which may throw up information relevant to people already under investigation. However, the volume of suspicious transaction reporting, delays in the distribution of information, and its means of dissemination (ie on paper) mitigate against this occurring (Gold and Levi, 1994). It is NCIS' responsibility to sift through the disclosures and either forward them to police units (including force Local Intelligence Officers) for further investigation, or to conduct independent investigation themselves.

Members of the FIUs studied conduct training classes for probationers to ensure that the majority of incoming officers are aware of the import of financial investigations, the evidence necessary to conduct them, and the basic parameters of confiscation legislation. They see this entrepreneurial mission as an important part of their work, to generate business from operational detectives as well as teaching them not to neglect financial intelligence. Some expressed envy at the Metropolitan Police system under which investigators attached to Territorial Offices accompany colleagues at selected searches, looking at all documentation on the premises for evidence that indicates bank and other accounts. At the minimum, they thought it would be useful (evidentially as well as for confiscation purposes) for officers to be told what to look for when searching homes. Such information could be a scrawled set of numbers on a piece of scrap paper, which could be deduced as account numbers in particular institutions by those familiar with such data. In at least one squad dealing with major investigations, case officers are currently instructed to raise questions regarding a defendant's finances during the initial interview of the defendant (under caution) so that the evidence can be used at trial and the financial side of the case can be developed fully by the time the trial begins. This shows the benefit of sound teamwork.

Some forces (such as South Yorkshire) provide helpful booklets outlining procedures for asset investigation. However, most training happens once staff are in post. 'On the job' training is made more difficult than in many other areas of police work, since (a) there may not be any more experienced officers around from whom to learn - a quarter of forces have fewer than two officers in the FIU - and (b) senior supervising officers may not have done this sort of work themselves and therefore would be unable to answer any technical queries. Moreover, for reasons of economy, formal training for FIUs has been cut from two weeks to one. Nevertheless, as in other police activities, officers from neighbouring forces are usually willing to help and CPS lawyers - discussed further below - likewise form a network of expertise on whom officers can draw. Financially trained officers frequently liaise with financial institutions about suspicious transaction reports, and are normally familiar with the appropriate procedures for getting information via Production Orders. Another part of their learned expertise which is almost as important is the knowledge, however frustrating, of what they *cannot* obtain. Among these listed frustrations is the inability to obtain legal aid application forms. The police would find this useful to compare and contrast statements made for the purposes of obtaining legal aid (e.g. about employment status) with those made in the course of a financial interview.

The FIUs work with the Crown Prosecution Service (CPS) and, in particular (and to their general preference and satisfaction), the Central Confiscation Unit (CCU) based at CPS headquarters to ensure that confiscation legislation is applied appropriately to particular cases. The CCU is comprised of one Grade 6 lawyer and seven other lawyers, as well as administrative and most notably accountancy staff who were very highly regarded by most of the officers interviewed. Although the CCU has a substantial volume of work, Customs & Excise were even more seriously under-staffed, with only three lawyers and three support staff.

The division of work between CPS branch prosecutors and CCU prosecutors is as follows. The CCU becomes involved when appearances in the High Court are necessary, such as when the Crown seeks restraint and charging orders. The CPS branch connected to a particular FIU is supposed to be the first port of call when a confiscation or forfeiture issue arises. The branch prosecutor may choose to contact the CCU and follow its advice. The branch prosecutor may also choose to allow the CCU to handle the case entirely or to retain control and prosecute the case without its help. In brief, the CCU is viewed by the police as an effective specialist unit, although many provincial forces find it inconvenient to deal with Restraint Orders in the London High Court only. Whilst there are advantages in having a small set of judges dealing with all the cases - and in practice, now, officers seldom need to travel to London, but rather communicate with the CCU by fax - this seems somewhat anachronistic. One (unintended) benefit is that restraint orders are left in the hands of the CCU and its customs equivalent which, by virtue of the number and range of cases with which they deal, are much more expert than a provincial branch prosecutor could be expected to be at this specialised task. For the most part, the police are confident that the CCU is well equipped to conduct confiscation-related actions successfully. Our survey indicated that confidence in CPS branch prosecutors is not as high. While some are knowledgeable about the relevant legislation, others appear to the police to be less so, and yet - the police state - branch prosecutors may refuse to consult the CCU. Confiscation is hardly a unique source of such 'turf battles', but we can see no rational reason for refusing to involve the CCU, except where the branch prosecutor has genuine expertise or does not intend to apply for restraint or confiscation on policy grounds.

It should be emphasised that the police have very little training in the compilation of affidavits, which are not simply witness statements but rather complex legal documents. In all other areas of law, affidavits tend to be settled by Counsel making the application - even the solicitor instructing Counsel will not draft them. Whilst the general quality of police-generated draft affidavits is very high the lawyers always have to settle the final version. This relates not just to substantive issues but also to apparently trivial issues such as grammatical style to which, because of their frequent contact with the judges who hear cases, the CCU and customs lawyers are more attuned than the police. Such local variations apply also to the form of Section 3 statements acceptable to different Crown Court judges though there, the expertise of the police is greater.

By way of contrast with the decentralised police FIUs, HM Customs and Excise has implemented the following structure to pursue confiscations and financial investigations, which reflects the more centralised structure of customs investigations generally. They have a small unit based in London, headed by a grade 6 lawyer, with two grade 7s and a support staff of three. They claim that their case load is about the same as the CCU, whose staff of eight lawyers and a larger administrative support group than customs are themselves hard pressed. It was agreed by police, CPS, and Customs & Excise investigators to whom we spoke that the customs confiscation unit were very competent and grossly overstretched. Unlike the police in some areas, who sometimes seek forfeiture of cash and moveable property under Section 27 of the Misuse of Drugs Act (MDA) 1971 or even more obscure older legislation (which can be the only way of removing offenders' assets if the charges are reduced to possession with intent to supply), Customs & Excise policy was to go for a confiscation order even where there were cash and vehicles that could be forfeited under the MDA or the Criminal Justice (International Co-operation) Act 1990, because they felt that this was the intention of the legislation. They found also that whereas under MDA forfeitures, they would have to spend time disposing of any assets seized which the court decided to award to them - such as elderly cars - under the confiscation legislation, this would be dealt with by receivers or by bailiffs acting for the magistrates' courts. Given limited time, this was felt to be more cost-effective.

The Customs & Excise unit deals principally (in about 80% of cases) with London Investigations Division (ID) cases; the rest come from 'Collections' in regions and from the smaller ID outposts there. Their relationships with officers are good, and they find it very convenient being close to the High Court. They are usually called in early, especially in VAT cases. Drugs cases can be more last-minute, partly because of the unpredictable speed with which they develop and break. Like the CPS, they do not like to get involved in pre-conviction administrative receivership cases (though accounting and legal costs are paid out of assets received later), but in 50-60 cases annually, they instruct receivers, mainly accounting firms with whom they negotiate (relatively) favourable rates. The CCU uses similar firms, though they expressed concern about the speed and efficiency, as well as the cost, of some of the receivers they have appointed in the past; their only real sanction is not to reappoint them in future.

Customs & Excise lawyers normally draft the orders in wide terms, so that if - during the arrest - they discover further accounts, they can just fax restraint orders to the banks. In a recent VAT fraud case, where the defendant owed approximately £500,000, the head of the Unit was able to utilise documentation about bank and other accounts, which he then used to restrain accounts about which he had no prior knowledge. Such 'hands-on' involvement has also been useful in police cases, though the 'accounts-receiver' would normally be a financial investigations officer rather than a lawyer. In VAT cases, where custodial sentences are usually very modest, confiscation orders take on a role as a substitute for the 'proper' punishment in the eyes of some investigators. With a fine, the initiative has to come from the judge, whereas confiscation arises from them. Moreover, there is no power to freeze assets to meet a fine. They also use confiscation orders in commercial pornography cases and to deal with the large-scale avoidance of duty on imported alcohol. At any one time, prosecuting solicitors in Customs & Excise have about 500 cases in progress. Some will have restraint orders, awaiting trial; others will have a confiscation order but be awaiting an appeal; while others are being dealt with by receivers.

In short, accessibility, flexibility, and familiarity both with procedures and with the people involved, enabling formal mechanisms for obtaining information and mutual legal assistance to be expedited, are essential to the efficient and effective conduct of confiscation proceedings. Nevertheless, no matter how great the competence of investigators and prosecutors, many frustrations are inevitable, given the exercise by defendants and their alleged beneficiaries of their 'human rights' not to have property confiscated before the exhaustion of appeals procedures.

6. Relationships between the police and other agencies

While this research has been primarily a review of policing policy and practice in the asset investigation area, given the inter-dependence of the police with a variety of other parties in the criminal justice process, it makes little sense to confine our comments to the police. However, in a short study of this kind into a very complex, substantial area, we have not been able to test independently every criticism made about other persons or institutions. Not all conflicts are reducible to 'bad PR': they may have an underlying real logic based on cultural differences, institutional or individual performance measures, and bureaucratic survival or development. We have interviewed a variety of people from organisations outside the police. However for the moment, we simply stress that what matters is police *perceptions* of the way that other parties within and outside the police operate, for it is these perceptions that take on a life of their own and affect practice.

Relationships within police forces

The research revealed that officers attached to FIUs felt isolated from many of their fellow officers (particularly at the upper management level) in the sense that many of these other officers appeared to have no real idea of what financial investigations entailed and the importance of these investigations. While specific forces felt that the management to whom they reported was supportive of their efforts, the vast majority were distressed at what they perceived as an "outdated" view held by these same managers that, unless an officer is locking up criminals, he or she is not doing "real" police work. Even where managers supported financial investigations in theory, police officers were sometimes frustrated by the lack of real understanding about what their work involved, and how time-consuming and thus officer-hour consuming it could be.

Though no officer complained about it, it is worth noting that more than one FIU that considered itself overworked, donated its members whenever important developments (e.g. arrests, surveillance, searches) needing more bodies occurred in cases being pursued by the drugs or fraud squad. The officers liked providing the help and saw their work as assisting in emergencies. It also improved their relationships with operational squads. As noted earlier, they were also able to look out for information relevant to the suspect's finances. However, while they were doing other tasks, financial investigation work was not being done. Moreover, it communicates a sense of priorities among the ranks of police responsible for allocating officer resources on a day-to-day basis.

One consequence of having few top ranking police officers know the details of financial investigations is that the FIUs (like some fraud squads) are left largely on their own. No one complained about the lack of supervision, and many of the officers who head FIUs felt that they had been selected because they had proven they could be trusted and did not need close supervision. However, it appeared obvious, during the course of the research, that some supervision by knowledgeable upper-ranking management - where these are available - might be needed to increase morale among the FIUs (since their bosses would know about and be expressing an interest in their work) and would also introduce some measure of objectivity in assessing the success of each FIU.

At a basic level, with few exceptions, the performance indicators used to evaluate FIUs' on-the-job performance bear little relation to the work done by financial investigators. For example, numbers of arrests, which may be highly relevant to assessing the work of some other police officers, have little place in the work of financial investigations. The numbers of cases dealt with is not particularly meaningful either, since complex cases may yield more, and may be (but are not necessarily) more 'important' than a large number of small cases. For example, South Yorkshire had ten times the number of confiscation orders as Greater Manchester, but their confiscation orders were only 60 per cent of GMP's total by value. We were, however, assured that the force was developing new guidelines (drafted specifically with financial investigators in mind). In addition, the statistics kept by each FIU monitors the work that the FIU actually does and tracks such things as how many production orders are issued, how many assets are restrained, and how many assets are ordered confiscated.

The core 'within-the-job' complaint of many FIUs will be familiar to police and Home Office administrators but is no less real for that. It is that there are 'just not enough bodies to go around'. This is tied in with their operational involvement in raids (which can involve lengthy waiting periods before the actual bust) and their work in processing (or, in some cases, not processing) suspicious transaction disclosures (Gold and Levi, 1994). In effect, with the exception of officers at the South East Regional Crime Squad, who refuse to handle financial disclosures which do not relate to their targets, there was very limited time for serious proactive work in building up financial profiles of 'target offenders'. The sheer volume of reactive enquiries occupied most officers. To the extent that crime squads generally shift towards targeting, this pattern may change, but it is has not yet occurred in FIUs to any great extent.

Relationships with Customs & Excise and Regional Crime Squads

Relationships between the police and customs in England and Wales are far from smooth. Indeed, we were told by a number of parties within and outside the police that difficulties commonly arise when the police and customs conduct joint investigations or have independent investigations with overlapping targets. While both customs and the police appear to work relatively well with the CPS, and, in particular, with the CCU, they sometimes compete with each other during joint investigations over such issues as who shall undertake Section 3 statements and whether seized funds should be placed in police or customs interest-bearing accounts pending conviction. Since the interest is part of the benefit to be confiscated, in principle, it is difficult to see why such conflicts should occur, unless they relate to property to be forfeited under the Misuse of Drugs Act, which can revert to the agency primarily responsible for the investigation and conviction. It is possible that the conflicts arise over accreditation of seizures to individual departments and thus performance measurement. Though HM Customs & Excise considered that a good relationship existed between them and the Regional Crime Squad officers after arrests on joint operations, when the RCS were handling the financial investigation side of the operation, police interviewed in England stated that customs officers were unwilling to reciprocate by divulging information about their own targets to the police. A similar view was expressed by some police about dealings with the Inland Revenue, but there is currently a statutory bar on communications from them about taxpayers' affairs.

It is not possible to assess from this study how universal these complaints are, whether the concerns about police corruption that partly underlie this alleged non-communication by customs have any validity, or whether the difficulties are simply a reflection of organisational cultures and performance indicators in conflict: an important problem where organisations compete for scarce resources. However, it should be noted that lack of communication can occur the other way.

The police are, it can be argued, out of their jurisdiction in situations involving the importation or exportation of drugs, since customs has priority in such cases. Several of the cases studied during the course of this research followed the same pattern. Even when police have informed customs about an ongoing case, which is expected to involve the importation of a significant quantity of drugs, customs allegedly will not tell the police if they are focusing on the same target. Thus, the research revealed a number of simultaneous investigations of the same criminal(s). Needless to say, this situation is, at least, inefficient and can be, if informants are involved, dangerous. It should be noted that similar problems of parallel investigation can occur where a force drugs squad and the Regional Crime Squad are investigating the same targets.

Other than lack of information sharing, customs and the police have different priorities. While the former, by mandate, must make seizures a priority, the latter are particularly interested in developing informants and following cases beyond the point of importation. According to the police, customs are unwilling to work a case in a way that might lead to the investigation of levels of criminality significantly higher up the organisational chain than the courier, if to do so might seriously risk losing the drugs seizure. Thus, if the police have been focusing on a dealer who controls an organisation, and gather intelligence indicating that a big shipment is due, customs will seize the shipment and arrest the courier rather than acceding to police requests to allow the shipment to enter the country so that it can be followed and leadership level criminals can be arrested. However, this is by no means a universal experience and customs do carry out a number of controlled delivery operations.

While relationships between the police and customs did not appear harmonious, the FIUs in most of the forces which were examined appeared to work fairly well with the Regional Crime Squads covering their areas. Though there were some tensions, police officers from the areas and the RCSs generally share information and divide up work fairly, on the basis of which office is best suited to pursue a particular case.

Relationships with the Inland Revenue

Under current law, the police must serve production orders on the Inland Revenue to obtain a defendant's tax information. While the Revenue are happy to comply (once an order has been served), proactive cooperation among the agencies may be the source of criticism and would be expected to lead to dismissal of Revenue officers. (The exception to this is in cases involving murder or treason, where the Inland Revenue's policy is to pass information to the police whether or not they are asked for it.) For instance, an Inland Revenue Inspector was criticised widely in the press for allegedly alerting the Serious Fraud Office to the suspected criminal dealings of at least one subject of a Revenue enquiry. Officially, communications between the Revenue and police are described as a one-way street.

An anecdote repeated frequently illustrates this point. The police were investigating, and ultimately arrested, an individual whom they suspected of trafficking in narcotics. During the course of the investigation, documents in the possession of the Inland Revenue were turned over to the police. These documents revealed that, for the past ten years, the defendant had reported to the Inland Revenue that his earnings arose from his activities as a drug trafficker. Since he had always paid a substantial tax bill, the Inland Revenue did not complain. The police were surprised and disappointed. A main plank of Inland Revenue resistance to changing this policy is that those drug dealers and other criminals who currently do pay are likely to desist, simply leaving the Exchequer much less well off.

Communication between police and tax authorities - as is common in the Netherlands and the US, for example - is always a controversial area in England. The exchange of information among various arms of the Crown would increase the likelihood that confiscation hearings would yield accurate information. The more information the prosecution knows about the defendant's assets, and the assets he has reported acquiring over time, the more difficult it would be for defendants to hide and, thereby, retain, their ill gotten gains.

Relationships with the Crown Prosecution Service

The role of the Central Confiscation Unit (CCU) is the object of some misunderstanding among some officers. It is policy that the CCU handles all High Court work (such as Restraint Orders) and is available for consultation on the preparation of Crown Court confiscation cases. In Criminal Justice Act 1988 cases (such as fraud and corruption), where the legislation requires the prosecutor to trigger the confiscation hearing, the CCU endeavours not only to assist the police but also to be present at the court hearing. However, the prosecution of confiscation proceedings always remains with the branch or headquarters Crown prosecutor who is handling the substantive case. Generally, participants in the confiscation process are satisfied with the work done by the CCU. However, some aspects of police relationships with the CCU raised concerns.

First, as is equally true of personnel in any organisation, the quality of lawyers at the CCU is not uniform. Though all legal and support staff were considered to be more than competent, which particular lawyer handles a case appears to make a big difference. Indeed, depending on which CCU lawyer the police speak with, a different threshold amount will be given as the minimum discretionary amount necessary for CCU involvement in a case.

Officers complained that sometimes the minimum amount quoted is £5,000 and other times it is £10,000 or even £15,000. These figures allegedly were given in trafficking cases, where statutes have never set forth a minimum requirement for confiscation to be permissible. It has not been the aim of this study to seek to examine the accuracy of the police reports. What matters practically is that the police believe these varied trigger points to be true, and modify their conduct of cases accordingly.

Another area of concern is the relationship between the CCU and the CPS branch prosecutor. Officers who have worked with the CCU tend to favour it and trust its advice. However, some police officers were interviewed who claimed that due to poor local relationships and/or their resentment towards 'headquarters', some branch prosecutors refused to involve the CCU, and because of their dependence upon prosecutors' co-operation generally, the police were sometimes reluctant to press their argument. Unless they do not intend to pursue a case to confiscation, there is no valid reason why a branch prosecutor should take this view, but the police saw this as a tension that they occasionally had to manage.

Other difficulties occurred regarding the London location of the CCU. While developing an affidavit for a restraint or charging order, provincial and non-London based forces cannot communicate with the CCU in person unless they travel to London. In part, this is simply a cultural problem of adjustment for the police from a personal contact-based method of dealing with issues to a more remote, hi-tech approach. But the absence of fax modems for inter-computer communications is a further inhibitor. In the view of the CCU, it is of no great benefit to have officers present at *ex parte* hearings.

In Merseyside, which is at least three hours from London, there is a High Court which, theoretically, could deal with restraint and confiscation matters now heard only in London. Likewise (though such requests would be few) in Cardiff, the High Court judge could deal with matters that arise in Dyfed-Powys as well as elsewhere in southern Wales. It is also possible, theoretically, to expand the jurisdiction of the provincial courts so that more of them, located throughout the country, can deal with confiscation matters. If there are more courts available to deal with such matters, then even cases involving assets worth less than an amount that the CCU is prepared to deal with might be brought to court. Since many of the cases that the police work with involve small-time dealers, and low sterling amounts, many of their defendants escape the confiscation provisions. Whether it is efficient to spend court and police time when only small amounts are involved is another question, determination of which needs to be linked to an assessment of the likely impact on the commission of further criminal activities. This is plainly an important area for police-CPS liaison and policy development, and reflects the more general difficulties of standardising operational practices and applying them to very different local environments.

One positive feature of holding hearings in London is that a specialist panel of judges, who know the legislation thoroughly, has developed. Accordingly, the levels of efficiency and fairness in the High Court proceedings held in London are high, and there is a significant chance that the judges will remember the cases from direct recall. Notwithstanding the inconvenience to the police, both CCU and customs prosecutors spoke favourably of the London focus (while acknowledging that it was more convenient for them personally), and expressed concern about what would happen post the CJA 1993, when Crown Court judges would deal with more confiscation issues than they had done in the past. Although it is easy to sympathise with the regional logic of the police position, this inconvenience of the London focus has to be balanced against the probable negative consequences of dispersing the CCU expertise to the CPS areas. CCU expertise arises from having staff dedicated to particular functions and having to cope with almost all the difficult cases related to those functions. In theory, it would be possible for the branch CPS lawyers (or exclusively the Special Case Officers) to deal locally with the simpler restraint and charging orders, while referring the more complicated ones to the CCU. In practice, given the need for rapid action, the delays (and potential organisational jealousies) that could arise while the branch prosecutor made that referral decision might mean that in the most complex (and perhaps the most important) cases, the service became slower than it is at present. One solution might be for the CCU itself to regionalise, as has been proposed for the Headquarters Fraud Divisions (Graham, 1994), or for the lawyer to visit the police and take the case to the regional High Court, but it is not clear that there are sufficient cases for this to be justifiable. The CCU derives benefits from having people along the corridor with whom they can discuss difficulties. This benefit would disappear if people are not in constant contact, as is likely if regionalisation took place.

There appears to be a lack of communication between the police and the Crown prosecutors regarding such simple matters as the dates of confiscation hearings. It is a reflection of the importance that the police attach to 'throughcare' in confiscation that they would normally 'keep an eye out' for the date of cases so that they did not find themselves surprised, or on leave, when cases in which they had an interest came up. It is difficult for other officers to 'pick up' a case when the FIU officer cannot attend, and in some forces - such as Dyfed-Powys and the City of London - there is only one officer in the unit. Numerous cases ended in less than satisfactory results, from a confiscation point of view, without any police notification or involvement. For example, cases were found in this study in which the police were able to answer questions that had been raised in court about a defendant's assets, but had not been informed that a hearing was taking place. In some of these cases, the court did not enter a confiscation order, or entered an order in an amount far less than that indicated in the Section 3 statement. Rather than seeking a delay of the hearing, or ensuring good communication beforehand, so that all parties with knowledge of the facts were present, the hearings often continued, with unsatisfactory results.

Relationships with prosecuting counsel

As a general rule, the police had little confidence in the prosecuting counsel with whom they had dealt. The distrust was on two fronts. First, they claimed, many counsel had very modest detailed knowledge of the law of confiscation. Second, counsel tended to plea bargain away assets that the police had included in their Section 3 statements. As explained above, in their statements the police detail **all** the identifiable benefit that - in their view - is properly attributed to the particular criminal activities conducted by the defendant (those under scrutiny at the time). As the practice has developed, the police specify the defendant's realisable assets in their statements as well. Though there is obviously scope for technical argument, these figures are meant to be absolute and accurate. They are not a starting point for negotiation about whether to include matrimonial homes, etc. As stated earlier, however, police officers saw nothing wrong with their entering into a similar bargaining dialogue with the offender earlier in the investigative process!

This study uncovered examples of cases in which counsel treat the figures included in statements as a launching pad for bargaining with the defence, presumably to settle the matter without a protracted hearing. The lack of trust is highlighted by the fact that, when the police are aware that a confiscation hearing is being held and view the case as significant, they attend the hearing to try to reduce the chance that counsel will plea bargain away the assets described in the statement. Though, ultimately, they may be powerless, some force FIUs stated that they took a very firm line with counsel. Others may be less vigorous. In some cases, counsel may decide on their own initiative not to trigger a non-drugs confiscation order at all. In one major spy trial in which it was acknowledged that the motive was greed rather than ideology, the prosecuting counsel set aside the careful police/CPS analysis of his benefit from crime and realisable assets, and did not request the court for a confiscation order, allegedly on the grounds that this would have distracted the court (and, one supposes, the media) from the lengthy prison sentence imposed for violation of the Official Secrets Act. This was despite what appears to be sound evidence of substantial benefit and realisable assets in excess of £20,000. The consequence is that these funds will be available for the offender on his eventual release. The CJA 1993 enables confiscation hearings to take place after sentence, so this sort of motivation for non-pursuit of confiscation will no longer be appropriate, if it ever was. In other non-drugs cases counts may be dropped in charge-bargaining which are essential to retain if the £10,000 minimum to trigger confiscations is to be reached. It appears to us that this may result from failure to consider the confiscation implications of such decisions. But whether or not that is so, the effect is to waste police time in conducting the financial investigation.

Not all bargaining is frowned upon by those participating in the confiscation process, however. Indeed, when the police and counsel feel certain that it would be easier to target certain assets, but not others, for purposes of confiscation orders, all parties readily and willingly participate in plea bargaining to arrive at an asset figure satisfactory to defence and prosecution alike, or even dispense altogether with the confiscation in favour of simple return of assets to victims. Several forces regarded this as a perfectly legitimate part of the process.

Though no bargaining is anticipated in the confiscation legislation, this study has shown that it occurs. The advent of such negotiations is objectionable to financial investigators only when they feel that their cases are traded away at greatly undervalued amounts behind their backs because, as they see it, their counsel or the trial judge either does not understand the legislation or cannot be bothered to spend time on the case. In other words, their quarrel is largely at the motivation behind the 'bargain' which undermines (and makes cost-ineffective) the time that they spent on the case. The de-motivating effect of such anticipated 'trades' is self-evident, though it is mitigated by the fact that not all counsel behave in this way. It might be countered that abilities at confiscation legislation may be a relevant criterion when selecting counsel. However, whatever other random and counsel availability factors may be in operation, the fact remains that counsel are selected by the branch prosecutors for general presentational skills. Knowledge of confiscation law is a bonus, and is pointless if the defendant is not convicted!

Relationships with the judiciary

Officers from a variety of countries stated there was judicial resistance to tough confiscation legislation, particularly where it involved making assumptions that all property was the proceeds of crime unless proven otherwise. In England, while there has developed a specialist panel of High Court judges who are fully familiar with restraint and confiscation legislation, interpretation and application of this legislation by Crown Court judges is by no means uniform and as the number of appellate cases indicates, the law is not infrequently interpreted and applied incorrectly. For example, it was claimed that some judges had applied provisions in the CJA 1993 which had not yet come into force, incorrectly assuming that because they appeared in Archbold (the practitioner's 'Bible'), they already applied! (see, more generally, Thomas, 1994.) Some of the cases studied revealed a lack of judicial familiarity with the intricacies of confiscation law which are outlined in the appendices. When independent counsel, too, are not knowledgeable on this area of the law, the work of the police and customs officers is wasted as well as the objectives of the legislation subverted.

One officer expressed a sophisticated perception of the confiscation issues thus:

> "Cases are often scaled down by Judges. In fact this occurs in the majority of cases. The fact remains that statements submitted under Section 3 are often done so without there being a satisfactory answer to questions by the defendant. It therefore follows that there may be an explanation for an income which the investigating officer is not aware of. Nonetheless the investigating officer must put his findings to the Court and if an explanation is forthcoming and cannot be faulted a reduction will follow. This is not a problem and is anticipated to some degree. The problems arise where the prosecution submits the Section 3 statement in good time but receives no declared answer from the defence prior to the DTOA hearing. If explanations are given at that hearing there is clearly no time in which to investigate any statement made by the defence. It is often the case that the explanation is not capable of investigation. In these cases the Judge often either gives the benefit of the doubt to the defendant or splits the difference: in other words, he reduces the amount to an amount which he believes is acceptable to both parties."

The latter line may be the pragmatic solution, but it causes resentment and wastes police efforts through alleged under-enforcement of the requirements on defendants. Consistent with the remarks quoted above, some reductions of prosecution-proposed confiscations are accepted by the police as understandable judicial responses to a plausible defence case:

- A case involving a Building Society account in the name of the accused jointly with his wife proved difficult in the linking of the assets in the account of the accused. His wife stated that she opened the account in joint names but had never informed her husband of its existence. He claimed that the monies in the account were his wife's and not from drug trafficking. The financial enquiry showed that the only person ever to use the account was the accused's wife and the Judge accepted this and did not make any confiscation order.

- In a drugs case, the benefit was assessed at approximately £78,000 using the assumption factors under Section 2 of the DTOA, but this was reduced to £28,000 by the Judge following a three-day confiscation hearing, during which the defendant (a self employed money lender) produced a number of witnesses satisfying the legitimacy of some of the funds.

However, as one might expect, there were some complaints about judicial acceptance of defendants' accounts, allegedly without substantiation:

- A cannabis dealer who had never worked had made cash credits to bank accounts totalling £17,000 over 3 years. The judge accepted his and his wife's (unsubstantiated) story that they had repaired vehicles and that his wife had run a small knitting machine business. The proposed order was reduced by 75 per cent.

7. Other practical difficulties encountered by the police

Computerised information

One area in which the current system works against the FIUs is that of computerisation. Some FIUs have only recently acquired computers and many have only one, which is not enough to keep the system current and also input old (previously handwritten) information. Indeed, none of the FIUs that were examined have all of their information (regarding past cases and intelligence) on computer. This appears to be one of the reasons that current statistics regarding confiscation-related activities are not available for each FIU. In one instance, it was possible to retrieve computerised data regarding confiscation cases only for the months from April to December 1993. As discussed below, without the ability to monitor activity in the area of confiscation, it is difficult to determine whether the confiscation programme in England is working effectively and, more specifically, whether the police FIUs play an efficient role in the overall scheme. If a hand search must be done each time a name comes up as a possible target, time is being wasted on what should be routine data checks. All of the FIUs proclaim the importance of intelligence and state that one of the services they provide is gathering intelligence (which may not be apparent in statistics that measure conviction rates). Since intelligence gathering appears to be one of the services provided by the FIUs, it would follow logically that access to such information is essential.

Where FIUs are fully computerised and relatively up-to-date in terms of adding previously handwritten financial and intelligence information into their databases, the way that police information is kept separately from NCIS information is not conducive to effective pursuit of confiscation cases. The newly commissioned ALERT system is likely to be of great benefit in this respect. In some forces, an 'urgent' request for information from INFOS requires the signature of a Detective Chief Inspector which, since that is well above the rank of direct supervisors in any force FIU, is a further source of delay. Any significant time lag in officers' ability to access financial data may severely undermine the effectiveness of the Crown ultimately to deprive criminals (to the fullest extent possible) of the proceeds of crime.

ACPO have proposed to remedy this by means of an asset marker placed on the Police National Computer (PNC). When Phoenix goes live during 1995, the standard information that is displayed when an individual's name is typed in will include confiscation-related information, such as whether that individual has an unsatisfied order pending against him. If one imagines a situation where a defendant who has not satisfied a confiscation order that has been pending against him is stopped shortly thereafter in a Rolls Royce, the uniform PC will then be able to feed that information in, which may lead to further confiscation and/or assessment of additional benefit.

Further, there is little standardisation among the different FIUs, in terms of acquiring and retaining financial data. One police force has tried to institute standardisation by designing and disseminating a manual describing and illustrating how the confiscation process works. The manual is distributed among all members of the force and the result has been the production of relatively uniform documents such as Section 3 statements. Nearly all FIUs keep standard forms on computer for all their regular documents, principally PACE and DTOA Production Orders, but not all FIUs use the same form. Hewson (1993) provides some model examples, and at least one Metropolitan Police area had very well designed forms.

In addition, while many FIUs keep track of the same data (such as Section 27 DTOA Production Orders served, number of NCIS disclosures, value of assets ordered confiscated in each year), there is little uniformity in the *manner* in which these statistics are kept. Without an official, standard policy about what information is essential, and how it should be kept, it is difficult to measure the productivity of each FIU.

The statistics themselves may not give a full picture of such productivity. For example, when each FIU records the number of NCIS disclosures, it is not clear from the statistics whether that means the number of disclosures received, the number investigated, the number distributed to other authorities for further investigation, or any other interpretation of such figures. When the number of pounds worth of assets ordered confiscated in one year are listed, that says nothing about how successful a particular case has been, since no flow data are kept about confiscation cases from start (investigation) to finish (through to enforcement). Instead, yearly totals are given which fail to track the success (or failure) of particular cases. Home Office criminal statistics are also compiled on a yearly basis and there is, similarly, no effort to trace cases from start to finish. This problem of measuring stocks versus flows is a major issue in long-lived serious crime cases, mainly fraud but also 'organised crime'.

The police are not alone in the resource problems they face. The geographical concentration of Investigations Division in London means that (in theory) there is better liaison than among the diverse police forces and Regional Crime Squads. However, Customs & Excise confiscation lawyers had no Information Technology at all initially, and even now, their equipment is very modest. From a social cost-benefit viewpoint, such resource starvation seems questionable.

Enforcing confiscation orders and the issue of performance indicators

As set forth above, under the law, once the police conduct a financial investigation (including travelling to jurisdictions where they believe a defendant's assets may be located) and a confiscation order has been entered by the Crown Court, the police officer's job is over and it is up to the magistrates' court (unless a receiver is sought by the prosecutor and appointed by the High Court) to enforce the order. Nevertheless, some officers are asked to and do assist the magistrates' courts in their collection efforts. Where the police have travelled to identify assets that are in a jurisdiction where further investigation of the assets is impractical and expensive, they will be the most knowledgeable about those assets, and it makes sense that the police work with the magistrates' courts to ensure that the Crown successfully collects those assets. However, though arguably enforcement of confiscation can be justified as crime prevention through incapacitation, this is not part of the officer's measured 'performance'. Even in the Regional Crime Squads, where data are collected on assets-per-officer, this is done only on the basis of the sums in the orders made, not the amounts actually collected. The confiscation order is treated as a fine for purposes of collection and is viewed as an outstanding debt which remains on the magistrates' books until the order is satisfied. It is open to doubt whether the authorities will pursue the tough line that prison sentences served in default will not expunge the order. If this does happen, failure to collect may become a greater administrative problem in the future. Performance indicators used to evaluate the performance of the magistrates' courts (and to determine the extent of the funds they will be allocated in the following year) include consideration of whether the courts have succeeded in collecting outstanding fines. Thus, the magistrates' courts are under pressure to collect the amounts specified in the confiscation orders.

There are certain problems with the system as it currently works. First, the value of a defendant's realisable assets, as determined by the police at the investigation stage, may be vastly different from their value at the time payment must be made. Depreciation, damage during storage, falling property market values, and inaccurate initial assessments all contribute to this divergence. In the US, such restrained 'perishables' may be sold even prior to the conviction, with procedures for compensation afterwards to acquitted defendants. Since the police know that they will not be responsible for ensuring collection of the amounts set forth in the orders, and they are encouraged by the system to get the largest confiscation order that is appropriate in the circumstances, there is no incentive to be cautious in the assessment of the value of a defendant's assets. Accordingly, the magistrates' courts may inherit a situation where the defendant cannot (and never really could) satisfy fully the obligations set forth in the confiscation order. Defendants' solicitors will not always heed the magistrates' clerks' pleas to seek variation of the order. If they do not, the magistrates' courts are helpless. Even if the parties petition the appropriate court, a great deal of judicial time and resources must be occupied to rectify this situation, which apparently occurs in the majority of cases. Under Section 17 of the Drug Trafficking Act 1994 (which came into force on 3 February 1995), a receiver will be able to apply to the High Court for a confiscation order to be varied downwards where there is insufficient realisable property to satisfy the order.

Magistrates' courts are responsible for enforcing confiscation orders because such orders are generally enforced in the same way as fines (one exception is that there is no power to remit all or part of a confiscation order). This means that magistrates' courts are able to make full use of Civil means of enforcement such as Distress Warrants, Garnishee Orders and the appointment of receivers.

Magistrates' courts are, by definition, neutral, adjudicatory bodies, with systemic incentives to keep outstanding debts at a minimum. Unlike the police, who have lived with the case from the time the investigation was initiated, or the Crown Court, which has heard all of the evidence in a case, the magistrates' courts are not privy to confiscation-related proceedings prior to enforcement and lack the factual background in each case. Therefore, these courts may not be in the best position, from a practical standpoint, to recover assets from defendants. Moreover, where, as under the current system, the magistrates' courts are under pressure to get the debts off their books and there are ways other than collection to diminish or expunge a defendant's confiscation obligations (such as serving a sentence in default for a CJA offence), the incentive system does not necessarily encourage *recovery* of assets. Prior to the new CJA, it actually made sense from a magistrates' court's viewpoint to clear its problem by getting the defendant to serve a default sentence rather than working on obtaining more money.

The net result can be a poor muddle, as in the following case:

•   L was a local builder and property speculator who would buy a property, improve it and sell it at a considerable profit. He detected an opening in the Local Authority improvement grant scheme whereby if he purchased the houses in other persons' names, he could get those persons to apply for a grant and thus the improvements became self funding and the profits considerably enhanced. This was a deception practised upon the Local Authority. Staged payments also helped L with his cash flow. By the time the deception was noticed L had amassed considerable property from the roll over of these profits.

A High Court order prohibited L from selling the houses and a year later, he was convicted and a confiscation order in the sum of approximately £68,000 was made. As the loser was the Local Authority, the compensation element - some £48,000 - was ordered to be paid out of the confiscation. £12,500 prosecution costs were also ordered. This was considered a very satisfactory result by the police.

However variations on the restraint were granted at various stages prior to conviction. On none of these occasions were the police asked to investigate any submissions from the defence. It is not known what efforts were made by the prosecution to enforce the Confiscation Order but it is known that the matter was eventually remitted to the committing magistrates' court for collection. Two years later L, who had not paid a penny of the confiscation, compensation or costs, was granted a certificate of inadequacy and the restraint order was discharged. The police were not asked to investigate any of the submissions of the defence in these matters either. The magistrates' court was told it could write off the confiscation order and therefore the compensation order, as it was integral. It did write this and the costs off. The prosecution appeared to have added the compensation to the confiscation sum - rather than pay one out of the other - and his assets were inadequate for this sum, but through a mistake, all the orders were permitted to lapse. The question as to why no steps appeared to have been taken to enforce the orders, in the period when L was known to have more than sufficient assets to satisfy any or all of the orders, was beyond the remit of the police.

This study has revealed that it is police officers who, over the course of the investigation and trial, have built up the strongest feelings about the possible impact of confiscation orders and commitment to their implementation. From the way that defendants fight the orders, all the police and CPS/Customs prosecutors who were asked deduce that the orders cause defendants pain, in a way that even prison sentences do not, particularly for 'hardened criminals'. Since, by the conclusion of the confiscation hearing, the police have spent more time than any other participant in the confiscation process chasing after the defendant, continued police involvement in the recovery of his assets may be appropriate. An opposing view is that the feelings the police have built up about particular offenders rules them out of this process, since they lack an appropriate level of objectivity and emotional detachment.

However, it must be acknowledged that such involvement in civil law is alien to normal police skills and culture, and that in their enthusiasm to ensure that suspected offenders do not benefit from their crimes, they may mistake the social obligations of bankers, etc. for legal obligations. For this reason, prosecutors felt that careful liaison and monitoring of police involvement was required, lest they made legal errors. Some of these difficulties will be eased by the comprehensive guidance on confiscation matters which is to be issued to the police, courts and others by the Home Office in 1995. Current texts, such as that by Mitchell et al (1992) are excellent detailed analyses of legislation, but what was needed was something simpler and more practical.

While the police monitor the total amounts of the orders they obtain and speak with enthusiasm about the large orders, neither they, nor any other participant in the system, compile data that follows confiscation cases through from beginning to end. (These data can be deduced from Customs & Excise statistics, but these do not automatically incorporate sums paid in previous financial years.) Indeed there are no accurate criminal statistics that reveal how much is actually recovered from defendants. Published statistics mirror the police statistics in compiling the total amounts reflected in the orders entered during each year. While the magistrates' courts report the amounts recovered to the Home Office, there are no accurate compilations of recovery resulting from non-trafficking crimes and the statistics that are compiled come complete with disclaimers regarding their accuracy. It is not surprising that, with so many different participants in the confiscation process, it is hard to measure success in each case. Each agency involved might respond that it is not their job to provide a 'cradle-to-grave' tracking process. However, until cases are accurately monitored from the investigation phase through the recovery phase (and recovery is noted as either real recovery or discharge through the serving of a sentence in default) then there is no way to assess the confiscation scheme now in place in England. It is recommended that such a monitoring system be put in place as soon as is practically possible.

Some key problems in applying the legislation

There appear to us to be three obstacles to effective, efficient confiscation of the proceeds of crime that even the new legislative provisions fail to remedy sufficiently.

(i) Investigative powers

In an ideal world, once the police have completed a financial investigation of a defendant, they should know all that there is to know about his finances. However, there appear to be frequent cases when a defendant proffers a story about particular assets that the financial investigation leaves the prosecution unable to rebut. Several illustrations were given concerning cases in which last-minute affidavits were offered from persons overseas testifying about their ownership of assets alleged to be the property of the defendant, which the trial judge simply accepted as true, though the police found them implausible. Effectively, once accepted in this way for the purposes of making the order, that was the end of the matter.

The legislation on non-drugs cases, even as amended by the new CJA 1993, leaves the police limited in their ability to conduct solely post-conviction enquiries regarding a defendant's assets. This barrier can leave the police and the prosecution ill-equipped to obtain orders of confiscation (or compensation) that reflect a defendant's benefits (and realisable benefits) from crime. Since it appears that it is often necessary to investigate the veracity of a defendant's asset-related statements *after* a conviction has been obtained and the merits of the case have been fully investigated and concluded, further legislation which would allow such investigation would assist the police in their role in the confiscation process. Section 15 of the Drug Trafficking Act 1994 (which came into force on 3 February 1995) allows the prosecutor to revise his assessment of an offender's benefit and apply to the Crown Court for an upwards variation of the original order.

(ii) Procedures for criminals' disclosure of assets

The 'right to silence' is a matter of some controversy, not least in the context of the European Convention on Human Rights. There is no obligation on the defendant to co-operate fully in helping the police or a receiver to trace the funds, nor to help to repatriate them (though to date, none have defied High Court orders to repatriate assets). The only 'weapon' is the prison sentence in lieu of payment. In the case involving convicted socialite Darius Guppy, his creditors have now made him bankrupt in order to assist their investigations into the whereabouts of his proceeds of insurance fraud, since Trustees in Bankruptcy have greater powers than financial investigators to require disclosure. Even there, no-one can be required to answer questions truthfully, though they can be punished if it can be proven that they have deliberately lied. On the other hand, perhaps excessive caution has been exercised by prosecutors in asking for the repatriation of non-liquid assets, such as homes or businesses overseas, which might be required to satisfy the confiscation order. There might be obstacles to this, for example exchange control laws in some developing countries which might prohibit the sending of capital overseas, but some of these could be overcome by mutual legal assistance treaties and other forms of international co-operation with countries such as Jamaica with which England has no current agreement. In non-drugs cases there are particular problems since, for example, despite the provisions of the 1959 Council of Europe Convention on Mutual Assistance in Criminal Matters, the Derbyshire Police had to exercise considerable ingenuity (without defendant co-operation) to deal with one particular fraud case.

(iii)   Third party rights

Though it does not relate directly to investigation conducted by the police, the confiscation legislation's provisions regarding the accommodation of the rights of third parties may obstruct the efforts of the Crown to meet fully the goals of the legislation. These provisions, of course, may be regarded as a vital safeguard, and the 1990 Council of Europe Confiscation Convention, for example, makes specific provision for them. Under previous law, and the law as amended by the new CJA 1993, unless the third party can satisfy the High Court at the restraint stage that there is no possibility that the asset will be made subject to confiscation or unless third parties are called as witnesses by the defence, the first opportunity for them to be heard is when (and if) a receiver is appointed, and/or when someone comes to seize the property that is in (potential) dispute. Given the very low numbers of cases involving ongoing businesses, this sort of dispute is rare. Third parties' rights most commonly arise in the context of disputes over matrimonial homes, and they are commonly brought up by the defendants themselves. It is (predictably) here that there is substantial dissatisfaction among police and prosecutors with the operation of confiscation provisions. It was not possible to ask all forces in how many cases matrimonial homes had not been seized when in officers' views, to do so would have been legally justifiable. However, this issue came up frequently in discussions with both police and prosecutors. Police (though not customs) considered that judges were too reluctant to impose a confiscation order whose effect would be to turn families out of their homes, even when - applying the assumptions in law - those homes must have been purchased by the proceeds of crime. One major force could recall no such cases at all, out of a large number of cases processed (though no figures were kept of the number of cases to which the argument applied). Customs agreed that judges (and they themselves) were happy to grant 'reasonable time' for families to move out of the matrimonial home, should it be sold to satisfy a confiscation order. While doubtless a humanitarian impulse - and possibly one which is less likely to provoke a return to crime to regain lifestyle after release - this completely fails to reflect the reparative principles underlying the legislation, ie that offenders should not profit from their crimes. In short, offenders (a) who spend their profits as they go along, and/or, to a lesser extent, (b) who use their funds to help to buy a home for their families and to furnish it expensively, are advantaged in practice by the application of the legislation. It remains to be seen whether the tougher provisions of the CJA 1993 will be applied in practice.

8. Ways forward

One of the aims of this study was to develop a good practice approach to confiscation based on observation, interviews and case studies, within the context of either normal or foreseeable conduct further downstream in the criminal justice process. Unfortunately no pattern could be discerned which was most likely to ensure successful results for confiscation purposes. Obvious factors improving the yield from confiscation included the extent to which judges, prosecuting counsel, and Crown prosecutors were well-versed in the relevant law, and defendants were co-operative. Case-specific phenomena not easily affected by those working in the system, such as the recovery of cash from the person of the defendant, also made for successful confiscation cases. The remainder of this chapter identifies a number of areas where improvements could be made to the systems in place in order to increase the yield of available confiscation powers.

Communication

Communication among all those participating in the confiscation process is essential to success. Informing the FIU early on in an investigation and keeping the FIU informed of upcoming court dates was valuable for FIU officers and ensured that the necessary financial investigation would be done. It was not, however, necessarily an indicator that the case itself would meet with success. Though it was outside the brief of this study to examine how best this might be done in practice, the police and customs must communicate to avoid wasteful duplication of effort and unnecessary expenditure of resources in conducting financial investigations.

Crown prosecutors must communicate with the police *and with counsel* to ensure that all of the important facts gathered throughout the course of the investigation are made known to counsel and, in turn, to the court. Moreover, communication between counsel and the police should ensure that cases are not negotiated away at rock bottom prices and that all of the evidence sought by the court during a confiscation hearing will be available to it. Whether, in the overall balance of a case, it is better to run the case and risk losing the conviction (and incurring extra expense) or trade off part or even all of the confiscation (as happens when non-drugs cases fall below £10,000 benefit or when drug offenders plead guilty to non-trafficking offences) is a broader issue which would repay debate. However, what is unacceptable is that prosecutors fail to take account of the confiscation consequences of their plea negotiations and make their own (and judges') lives easier by failing to press confiscation issues. Financial investigators' time could be saved by devoting minimal effort to those cases where this was likely to occur.

Policy-makers and those drafting legislation must continue to communicate with those responsible for implementing the legislation on a day-to-day basis - including operational detectives of modest rank - to ensure that there are no practical holes causing unnecessary obstacles for those working to attain the goals underlying confiscation legislation. Not only can practical input from the police or the magistrates' clerk ensure increased efficiency, but it is also helpful for boosting morale and encouraging participants in the system to work together to meet their goals.

A corollary to communication among the various participants in the confiscation process is an effort to streamline the process and, thus, either pare down the numbers of participants or, at least, designate one participant whose job it is to monitor each confiscation case through the recovery-of-assets phase. One option would be to consider removing magistrates' courts from the process, and leave enforcement of confiscation to the police service, who would be funded accordingly. Such a system of so-called through care would ensure that cases are not left to languish unenforced or, at least, unmonitored. One policy issue that must be determined clearly is the balance - reflected in performance indicators - between the distinct objectives of (1) maximising sums recovered from offenders, and (2) recovering offenders' assets only if they are estimated to exceed the estimated costs of recovery. A 'cradle to grave' approach would make it easier to keep track of the outcome of each case, not only in terms of orders entered but also in terms of assets recovered. Accurate, uniform statistics are essential to any proper assessment of police work in the area of confiscation.

Standardisation

Our research revealed that each FIU is run somewhat differently and that the documents submitted to the High Court and Crown Courts vary also. Standardisation throughout the police service in the way that financial investigations are monitored and in the documents produced by the FIUs would improve the system in a number of ways.

If the judges and magistrates reviewing the documentation knew precisely where, in each submission, to find a particular issue addressed, the process would become more efficient and predictable. Since there was a wide disparity in the ways the courts applied the law of confiscation to individual cases, it would be helpful to include citations to the relevant law in the submissions. Such inclusions would minimise the number of times that lawyers from both sides and the presiding judge would be unaware of the appropriate law. Obviously, the police would have to work with the CPS and, in particular, with the CCU to get the correct law incorporated into standard submissions papers but, presumably, once standardisation does occur, subsequent alterations will be a matter of fine tuning rather than creating from whole cloth.

Although standard forms are produced by the Lord Chancellor's Department, further standardisation within the police service would assist the FIUs in reviewing work done by other officers (both in the FIU and those performing other duties). If each officer knew precisely where to include each particular type of information, then non-FIU officers could easily follow the format to do their own simple Section 3 statements (and would know which documents to attach and where). In addition, FIUs and the officers with whom they work would not have to waste time first reading through all of the papers to determine what format a particular officer was following and would, instead, know exactly where to look for whatever information is necessary at the time.

Presenting a uniform approach would assist the CPS and CCU lawyers who need to evaluate statements and other documents for their evidential value (to determine what is appropriate for submission in court). If all restraint and charging affidavits follow the same format, and the format is one that is devised with input from the CPS (including the CCU) at the outset, this should alleviate the need for rewriting and refaxing documents when speed is essential. It would also diminish complaints that each Crown prosecutor has his or her own particular approach, which makes it difficult for the police to get it right the first time. Standardisation, thus, should increase efficiency and accuracy and should decrease delays at crucial phases of the confiscation process, particularly restraint orders, where immediate action is necessary.

Training

On a related note, force-wide training in the area of financial investigations, with a focus on confiscation, would be desirable. While certain members of FIUs throughout the country lecture some members of their forces, it does not appear that there is a set method of training all officers in the area of financial investigation in general and confiscation in particular. Rather, if one especially organised and forward-thinking detective sergeant has made a point of lecturing (usually junior) officers, then those officers will be familiar with aspects of the work done by the FIU in that area and may be energised to pursue those dimensions of their enquiries. However, that is no guarantee that all incoming or even senior ranking officers will have had any training in the area of financial investigations. On the other hand, some officers felt that their own training had been largely wasted, inasmuch as they did not do any confiscation work for some time thereafter, and the 'message' was not reinforced by immediate experience. This indicates the problem of matching people to training at the right time, when the numbers requiring training are high enough only to justify periodic courses.

This study showed that, where an FIU works very closely with one group of officers, the FIU feels confident that that group has been well-trained enough to collect all relevant financial evidence during the course of an investigation. For example, when a drugs squad that works closely with the FIU conducts a search of a defendant's residence, the FIU does not feel compelled to accompany the squad and participate in the search. However, when a squad with whom the FIU does not work closely conducts a search, the FIU comes along. Training is expensive (both in real and opportunity cost terms), but there seems to be no reason why all squads could not be trained to conduct searches that satisfied the needs of the financial investigators. It would simply be a matter of training all officers to be aware of the need for certain types of evidence, and to pass on this information promptly to financial investigators, so that they can request prosecutors to apply to the High Court to freeze accounts before they are emptied. This awareness could be introduced at training sessions for all officers. In addition, an apprenticeship period during which either an FIU officer trained other officers on the job or the other officers spent time with an FIU might prove useful. At the very least, the non-FIU officers would develop an understanding about the types of evidence the FIU officer needs. At best, officers might be more self-reliant in handling confiscation matters and the FIUs could, like the CCU, develop more fully as specialist units. This relates to the wider question of specialisation in police functions. There is a negligible career development structure in financial investigation, and though some officers' dynamism drops over time, this (like fraud) is certainly an area where high turnover of competent staff is undesirable for efficient functioning.

Co-operation with the private sector

Inevitably, there are tensions when the police or customs wish accounts to be frozen pending the obtaining of a restraint order. Bankers who are willing to co-operate thereby place themselves at risk of being sued by the account-holder, particularly if the restraint order is not applied for or is not granted, factors which are outside the control of the investigators. It is difficult to see what could be done about this problem, short of granting controversial 'hot pursuit' powers to the police either at the potential expense of the taxpayer or without redress for those thereby wrongfully harmed.

The Money-Laundering Regulations 1993 should make it more difficult for offenders to open up accounts in false identities, though they can still use nominees with genuine identities to do so on their behalf. Given the multiplicity of financial institutions in various parts of the country, it would ease the task of investigators and prosecutors if there were some centralised means of issuing the equivalent of an 'all ports' message to all financial institutions - principally banks and building societies - holding accounts in specified names, to enable them to be frozen and/or disclosed. Despite the considerable progress that has been made through the British Bankers' Association towards police-bank co-operation, such centralised assistance is not yet in place across the board. Furthermore, the incomplete centralisation and computerisation of accounts means that banks and building societies vary in the ease with which they can implement procedures to 'search out' those accounts of persons subject to confiscation proceedings that are not already known to the police but that are in the offenders' genuine names. This would help to close the information circuit, particularly as offenders become more adept at hiding financial details, though there is a limit to the extent that they can do so without risking loss of control over their funds themselves.

Other strategic issues

The analysis of effectiveness and efficiency in detective functions can only meaningfully take place within a broader context of downstream decision-making by public prosecutors, independent counsel, judges, and jurors. However thorough and competent a financial investigation is, it has no clear value if no-one acts on it fully. This study found that the utilisation of such investigations by prosecutors, judges and asset collection officials is both highly variable and largely unpredictable, in the sense that one seldom knows in advance who will be dealing with the 'product' of the financial investigation, and in what way they will deal with it. This makes rational planning difficult and the reason for the wide perspective adopted in this report. It must be emphasised that unless the way they deal with confiscation matters becomes more important to counsel, there is little chance of dramatic improvement in the effectiveness of financial investigation for confiscation purposes. Apart from the osmotic growth in expertise in this area, the only way this would be likely to be achieved would be as part of the systematic monitoring of counsel's performance, for example with box markings for competence which would then become an important criterion for re-employment by the CPS or Customs & Excise. This doubtless would be represented as an attack on the independence of the Bar, but - done properly, perhaps with some opportunity to defend one's performance - it simply represents a more systematic way of evaluating the costs and benefits of public expenditure. Indeed, customs currently maintain lists of experienced barristers whom they employ for such specialist work. The lists are graded A-C on the basis of experience, and a separate list for Queens' Counsel is also maintained. Lawyers can rise up or fall down the list, based on judgments of performance.

This research has had to draw some artificial boundaries between the sub-disciplines of asset investigation, seizure, and confiscation within the framework of general financial intelligence functions. It has not sought to discuss the weight which the Home Office attaches to confiscation efforts and the broad strategic issues which need to be addressed, such as whether anti-drugs trafficking and thus confiscation measures should be targeted proportionately more at the high-level distributors than they are at the moment or whether - as the data examined in this study suggest is currently the case - they should continue to focus on street-level, relatively asset-less, dealers. Under the Drug Trafficking Act 1994 it will no longer be mandatory for the courts to make a confiscation order in all drugs cases where a defendant has benefitted from trafficking. The intention is that small, unviable cases where people deal largely to feed their own habit will be weeded out of the system. So long as the latter strategy predominates, it would be unwise to expect much from confiscation legislation, no matter how efficient the police became.

Other salient strategic issues include whether the current baseline for *non-drugs* confiscations - £10,000 - should be retained or should fall. The very modest number of non-drugs 'crime for profit' confiscation orders reflects not only widespread ignorance that compensation and confiscation can be combined compatibly, but also the difficulty that the police and prosecutors have in generating convictions involving more than £10,000 in realisable benefits from crime to convicted persons. This should be remedied in practice by Sir John Hannam's Proceeds of Crime Bill 1995. If the same retrospective criteria that are currently used in drugs cases were applied to fraud, corruption and other cases of crime for gain, this might have a considerable impact on those who currently feel secure in enjoying the benefits of past crimes, including undeclared income from legitimate activities for which they otherwise would not have needed to account. However, overall, this study suggests that it may not be plausible, given the sort of people who are convicted, for the confiscation process to obtain vastly more funds than it does at present. The comparison with the United States - however invigorating to detectives as a goal to aim for - may be misleading, reflecting as it does not only the very different legislative environment, but also the differences in scale and organisation of crime there. Evidence from Australia, Canada, and the Netherlands, for example, suggests a scale of financial returns from confiscation and forfeiture, even when calculated prior to enforcement costs, that is not far removed from those obtained in the UK. As has been pointed out, like so many other police functions, the 'success' of financial investigations work depends substantially on factors outside the control of the police. However, these **are** important functions, and consideration should be given to how responsibility - and credit - for implementing them should best be rationalised. Any such rationalisation must remain compatible with the proactive financial investigative work done by the Regional Crime Squads and metropolitan forces, and avoid too narrow a focus on the financial cost-benefit of each individual investigation which might frustrate some of the broader reparative and deterrent/incapacitative purposes of the legislation.

Many police officers were enthusiastic about the potentially motivating effects on their unit or their force of retaining the assets that 'they' (or rather, the prosecution and enforcement institutions, on the basis of their work) had confiscated. There are powerful 'slippery-slope' arguments against 'hypothecation', ie tying the allocation of income to specific public sector functions. In Australia, the proceeds from domestic as well as from international confiscation orders are put into a national fund which disburses funds to drugs prevention initiatives as well as to force units, who bid for technological and other facilities that are not available from normal budgetary headings. This is also - contrary to folklore within the UK police service - formally the case in the US. While the Australian system seems to avoid some of the potential real and perceived excesses of US-style forfeiture funding, there are objections to this approach (see Fisse et al, 1992). In any case, their income from confiscation has not been great, though it is higher than that in England in relation to their population. Some may question why the police should propose that resources spent on financial investigation are reimbursed directly to them, when other, financially unproductive police functions are not. Given other 'performance pressures', however, there seems little likelihood of persuading senior officers to devote more of their scarce resources to confiscation-related work unless there is some greater direct ratio of effort to reward *for their force* than exists at present. This argument may also apply to HM Customs & Excise, where confiscation work is sometimes thought to divert resources which could be used in revenue collection, though customs officers, like the police, *hope* that their confiscation activities will generate more resources in the future than would otherwise have occurred.

This report has suggested some ways in which the existing process of investigating and dealing with confiscation issues could be improved, but there remain some larger questions about inter-agency collaboration and how that is to be formally rewarded (or its absence penalised), which are important for policy-makers. It is hoped, however, that this report will help to bring some clarity of thinking, as well as some carefully assembled information, to the debate over this important area of policing and penal policy.

References

Adler, P. (1993), *Wheeling and Dealing, 2nd ed.* New York: Columbia U.P.

Ashworth, A. (1992), *Sentencing and Criminal Justice*, London: Weidenfeld & Nicholson.

Audit Commission (1993), *Helping with Enquiries*, London: HMSO.

British Retail Consortium (1994), *Retail Crime Costs*, London: British Retail Consortium.

Dorn, N., Murji, K. and South, N. (1992), *Traffickers*, London: Routledge.

Duyne, P. van (1994), 'Estimates in Fog', *Journal of Asset Protection*, 2(1), 58-76.

Fagan, J. (1994), 'Do criminal sanctions deter drug crimes?' in Mackenzie and Uchida (eds.), *Drugs and Crime*.

Financial Crimes Enforcement Network (1992), *An Assessment of Narcotics-Related Money Laundering*, Washington, D.C.: US Treasury.

Fisse, B., Fraser, D. and Coss, G. (eds) (1992), *The Money Trail*, Sydney: the Law Book Co.

Gold, M. and Levi, M. (1994), *Money Laundering in the UK: an Appraisal of Suspicion-Based Transaction Reporting*, London: Police Foundation.

Graham, J. (1994), *Review of the Handling of Serious Fraud*, London: Attorney-General's Chambers.

Hewson, B. (1993), *Seizure of Confidential Material: PACE Special Procedure*, London: Butterworths.

ISDD (1993), *Drug Misuse in Britain, 1992*, London: Institute for the Study of Drug Dependence.

Karchmer, C. (1985), 'Money laundering and the organized underworld', in H. Alexander and G. Caiden (eds.) *The Politics and Economics of Organized Crime*, Lexington: Lexington Books.

Levi, M. (1981), *The Phantom Capitalists: the Organisation and Control of Long-Firm Fraud*, Aldershot: Gower.

Levi, M. (1991), *Customer Confidentiality, Money Laundering, and Police-Bank Relationships*, London: Police Foundation.

Levi, M. (1993), *The Investigation, Prosecution and Trial of Serious Fraud*, Royal Commission on Criminal Justice Research Study No.14, London: HMSO.

Levi, M. and Osofsky, L. (1994), 'The end of the money trail: Confiscating the proceeds of crime', in R. Parlour (ed.) *The International Handbook of Money-Laundering Law and Practice*, London: Butterworths.

Levi, M. and Pithouse, A. (forthcoming), *The Victims of Fraud*, Oxford: Oxford University Press.

Maguire, M. (1982), *Burglary in a Dwelling*, Aldershot: Gower.

Mitchell, A., Hinton, N. and Taylor, S. (1992), *Confiscation*, London: Sweet and Maxwell.

Mitchell, A. and Hinton N. (1994), 'Confiscation inquiries - what the Dickens?', *Journal of Criminal Law*, 201-208.

Mackenzie, D. and Uchida, C. (1994), *Drugs and Crime: Evaluating Public Policy Initiatives*, Thousand Oaks: Sage.

Mayhew, P., Maung, A. and Mirrlees-Black, C. (1993), *The 1992 British Crime Survey*, London: HMSO.

Scottish Affairs Committee (1994), *Drug Abuse in Scotland, Vol.1*, First Report, London: House of Commons, 1993-94, 62-1.

Senate (1993), *Checking the Cash: a Report on the Effectiveness of the Financial Transaction Reports Act 1988*, Canberra: Senate Standing Committee on Legal and Constitutional Affairs.

Serious Fraud Office (1994), *Serious Fraud Office*, Sixth Annual Report, London: HMSO.

Shover, N. and Honaker, D. (1992), 'The socially bounded decision-making of persistent property offenders', *Howard Journal of Criminal Justice, 31(4)*, 276-293.

Sutton, M. and Maynard, A. (1992), *What is the Size and Nature of the 'Drug' Problem in the UK?*, Yartic Occasional Paper 3, York: Centre for Health Economics.

Sutton, M. and Maynard, A. (1994), *Trends in the Cost-Effectiveness of Enforcement Activity in the Illicit Heroin Market, 1979-1990*, Yartic Occasional Paper 4, York: Centre for Health Economics.

Thomas, D. (1982), *Current Sentencing Practice*, updated looseleaf, London: Sweet & Maxwell.

Thomas, D. (1994), 'The Criminal Justice Act 1993: (1) Confiscation orders and drug trafficking', *Criminal Law Review*, 93-100.

US government (1992), *International Narcotics Control Strategy Report*, Washington, D.C.

Wright, A., Waymont, A. and Gregory F. (1993), *Drugs Squads: Law Enforcement Strategies and Intelligence in England and Wales*, London: Police Foundation.

Appendix 1

Illustrations of investigative problems in drugs profit confiscation cases

- The defendant, Ms. 0 was convicted of possessing £50,000 worth of heroin and sentenced to four years imprisonment. The sentencing court ordered that £53,143 be confiscated from the defendant and that she serve two years in default. Her prison term was imposed on January 28, 1992; the confiscation order was entered on December 17, 1991. The defendant's assets include £6,700 in cash found in the defendant's house at the time of her arrest, and substantial cash deposits had been made in bank and building society accounts.

  The defendant's appeal rests on her assertion that there "was no evidence and/or insufficient evidence for the learned Judge to be sure that the appellant had been dealing in drugs for the previous 6 years." As the provisions of the DTOA make clear, this 6-years-prior-to-the-date-of-drug-dealing assumption is one that the sentencing court may make, unless the defendant can show otherwise. Thus, it appears that the claim is not likely to succeed.

  Nonetheless, because the defendant has lodged an appeal, and the appellate court has not yet resolved the matter, the confiscation order may not be enforced and the sentence in default may not yet be served. The defendant has completed her jail sentence and is back on the street. To get her to serve her default sentence years after she has completed her jail time does not appear to be the intention of the drafters of the confiscation legislation. Moreover, finding a defendant who has been released from prison, rearresting such a person, and transporting him or her back to jail appears to be a waste of time and money. This case reflects problems in the speed of appeals, including the filtering process for them.

- This case illustrates the problems that can arise when a judge, unsolicited by either party, becomes highly active in a case. Here, the judge recalculated the amount of benefit acquired by the defendant in a DTOA case, without any prompting from the defence.

  The defendant pleaded guilty to one count of possession with intent to supply and two straight possession counts (cocaine and cannabis). One month later, the court held a Section Three hearing. At the hearing, the judge posited, without any prompting from the defence, that certain figures "may have been doubly counted." These figures pertained to a Nat West Bank Account and an Abbey National

Building Society Account. As the judge then explained, what he meant was that figures listed in the expenditure column of the Unit's Section Three statement could have been paid from funds from either account (though we are uncertain as to why that is significant). As a result of this perceived double counting, the judge took all of the cash figures out of the benefit calculus. The benefit figure went from £6,181.27 to zero. In other words, in the judge's view, the defendant did not benefit from drug trafficking at all.

The judge then insisted that £5,000 that was listed as "family allowance" be included as part of the defendant's realisable assets. However, the judge took no account of the fact that this money was used to support a family of two adults and four children over a period of three years. The defence sought an adjournment so that it could consult with the prosecution. The parties then agreed that H had benefitted from drug trafficking and that this benefit consisted of two £900 drug purchases, to which H had admitted, and £1,350 in cash that was recovered by the police during the search of H's home.

The parties returned to court and presented the judge with an agreed proposal. The sum of £3,150 (the agreed benefit amount) was to be confiscated. H would pay with the £1,350 cash and other assets valued at £1,800. The court agreed to enter an order reflecting this arrangement. H was sentenced to 15 months in jail and was given a sentence in default (if the £1,800 was not paid) of 7 weeks imprisonment. H agreed to pay the recovered £1,350 to satisfy the confiscation order.

• The defendant C was arrested with 5 ounces of heroin in 1992. At the time of his arrest, he had £3,080 in his socks. The Unit was brought into the case by the drug squad to which it is attached after the defendant's arrest. The money recovered from the defendant was restrained; accordingly, the CPS became involved in the case.

Financial investigation revealed that the defendant had sent £40,000 back to Turkey, to his brother. The Unit went to Turkey to see where the money went and to get a statement from the brother. The brother stuck by his defence that he had sent the defendant leather jackets to sell and that the defendant had sent the money for the jackets back to the brother. The brother was only able to document the purchase of 19 jackets, which would hardly have netted £40,000. The trip to Istanbul was not a success in that the police were not able to trace where the money went. Despite the defence, the defendant was convicted in 1994. The reason the case took so long to come to trial (which allowed the Unit sufficient time to investigate) is because the defendant is an addict who failed to appear in court, time and again.

The figures tendered by the police for confiscation purposes included £18,000 benefit and £5,000 in assets. During the time that the defendant's money was restrained, the court allowed the defendant £150 each month for living expenses. Because of the defendant's alleged illness, the case was postponed, and the moneys 'restrained' in the bank account were all spent by the time the confiscation order came to be imposed. Consequently, the only funds confiscated were those found on him when arrested.

- Following his arrest, B was convicted of conspiracy to produce amphet amine. He was sentenced to 15 years in jail. After he was arrested, the police sought a restraint order and the defendant's caravan, worth about £19,000, was restrained. In the Section Three statement, the police estimated B's benefit at £6,000,000 based on the potential street value of amphetamine capable of being produced at B's laboratory. At the time B was sentenced, the parties agreed that B's only asset was the vehicle worth £19,000; the court ordered confiscation in that amount.

After B had served some of his sentence, he tried to open a bank account in jail. B wanted to deposit £142,000 in cash, money that he allegedly did not have at the time of the confiscation hearing. Once the Unit received this information, it approached the court to have the confiscation order changed. The judge had no notes regarding his confiscation decision and informed the Crown that he needed a transcript of the hearing to determine the stated benefit amount and to evaluate the representations made by B at the time of the hearing, but the cost of making the transcript was a problem both for the police and the CPS, since they do not benefit from the order!

- A woman was arrested at her home address following the execution of a search warrant. Inside was found Cannabis Resin, Herbal Cannabis and Amphetamine Sulphate having a street value of approx. £4000. Also seized was £400 cash and the usual items used for cutting and packaging drugs. The woman and her husband had been suspected of drug dealing for some time. The defendant alleged that she and her husband ran a car sales business and the £400 was part of that business. During interview the defendant admitted to supplying drugs for at least

8 to 9 months. She had been doing so on behalf of another who she declined to name, in order to pay off a debt which she owed to them. During the course of the interview she stated her debt to this person was between £3700 and £4000, and then altered it to £28000. She stated she passed the money earned from the sale of the drugs directly to the supplier. It was difficult to establish the exact amount of benefit but the minimum was established at £22,568. Enquiries revealed that both the defendant and her husband were claiming unemployment benefit and there was no evidence of any vehicle trade. All their finances were in cash.

The defendant appeared before the Court and was given a suspended sentence. Officers from the Financial Investigation Unit were not called to give evidence in the trial or the DTOA hearing and were not informed of the dates of such hearings. The Judge determined that there was "no benefit" in this case. It is difficult in this case to see how the above decision could have been reached based on the admissions of the defendant.

Appendix 2

Illustrations of investigative problems in non-drugs profit confiscation cases

- The case involves a customs officer who was charged with stealing cash from mail that arrives through the international mail system (which is monitored by customs). The defendant allegedly stole primarily Dutch guilders and German marks. He took £200 during the course of controlled deliveries and was believed to have stolen about £125,000 cash over the past three years. The cash ultimately made its way to a betting agency. The £125,000 figure was derived from betting-related deposits that exceeded the defendant's legitimate salary.

  After a covert investigation, there were four controlled deliveries, each of which was represented by a separate count. However, these deliveries totalled only £200, a small fraction of the amount the defendant purportedly stole over the years. To represent the additional £125,000 in the indictment, the police requested a fifth count, charging an overall course of conduct because, under non-drugs confiscation law, funds that may be the subject of confiscation must be linked to particular charges. In the end, this charge was not pursued and because - allegedly as part of the plea bargain - the counts were not put on the basis that they formed part of a systematic course of conduct, no confiscation order was applied for. This case illustrates the difficulties posed in non-drugs cases by the inability to make the assumptions that assets derive from crime unless demonstrated otherwise. The problem is dealt with in Sir John Hannam's Proceeds of Crime Bill.

- In an immigration and mortgage fraud brought under the CJA 1988, £2,500,000 in assets were restrained and, at the conclusion of the case, there was only £26,000 left. While the case was pending, the defendant obtained the release of over £2,000,000 to pay for private hospital fees (where he apparently mounted an insanity defence). Finally, the court found the defendant was not fit to plead and the case against the defendant was effectively dismissed, and the restraint order lifted.

- In 1990 a builder was prosecuted for a series of building society mortgage frauds which he had committed over a number of years. It was established that owing to the frauds and the rapid rise in house prices during the relevant period he had made illegal profits in the region of £100,000. This was covered by the equity in his current address which had also been the subject of a mortgage fraud. A restraint order was successfully obtained in respect of the dwelling. At the subsequent trial, the defendant pleaded guilty and the Court agreed with the general prosecution argument. However, the judge declined to grant a confiscation order on the grounds that such action would render the accused's children homeless. In the event the accused kept his home and thereby profited by his actions. Under Sir John Hannam's Proceeds of Crime Bill, however, the court will lose its discretion to make a confiscation order under the Criminal Justice Act 1988 for an amount lower than the defendant's benefit, or the amount of realisable property available for confiscation.

- The defendant was arrested and charged with conspiracy to defraud concerning a large scale motor car "ringing " operation. He was assessed as having benefitted in the sum of £51,000. In addition an application for a compensation order was to be made in the sum of £48,000. It was anticipated that if the Court made a confiscation order in the sum of £51,000, then the compensation could be met out of this sum. Without reference to the police an agreement was reached between prosecution and defence barristers whereby the prosecution would not make an application to the Judge for a confiscation order on production of a disclaimer signed by the defendant for certain items of property, which were much less than the value of his realisable assets. The defendant pleaded guilty, and no application was made for a confiscation order.

- A husband and wife were arrested and charged with offences of deception concerning the obtaining of mortgages for the purchase of property by fraud. They were jointly assessed as having benefitted from these activities in the sum of £220,000. Realisable assets were identified in the region of £250,000, which had been made subject of a restraint order. The defendants were convicted and an application for a confiscation order was made to the Judge during a separate two-day hearing. The Judge finally declined to make an order owing to a £1 million debt owed by the defendant to the Inland Revenue whom he felt were best able to strip assets. Up to this point the Inland Revenue had taken 6 years to investigate the defendant. It was later unofficially established that due to continuing difficulties in recovering the debt owed, the debt was written off. Undr Sir John Hannam's Proceeds of Crime Bill, however, the court will be required to make a confiscation order where the prosecutor tenders notice.

- This three year bribery investigation involving oil rigs in the North Sea was one of only two confiscation orders in Serious Fraud Office cases to date. (The other involved the Wallace Smith Trust case, ending in confiscation of £49,000 during 1994.) The bribes were paid so that various contractors would receive inside information about the bidding process, thereby enabling them to obtain contracts for construction work. Construction companies worked through middle men (who were prosecuted) to obtain information from insiders employed by the companies who were seeking bids for the work. Four separate prosecutions arose from the investigation. In several of the prosecutions, the SFO charged both the middle men and the insiders. The SFO decided that there was insufficient evidence to prosecute the companies that *paid* the bribes, though their evidence was not needed to secure the convictions of the others.

Of the five prosecutions, two involved the confiscation of assets. The facts in this set of cases made them well-suited for confiscation, since all of the bribe paying companies got the contracts they sought and it is difficult to imagine a sensible scheme whereby those companies that did not get contracts (and who could say exactly why their bids were not accepted?) could be compensated because they were disadvantaged during the bidding process. (Furthermore, what criteria would be used to fix the amount of the damages, if awarded? This is an issue better suited to the civil courts.)

The first case was tried in January 1993 and involved defendants Szrajber and Sorelli. Both received three-year sentences upon conviction. Each was given terms of five years in default (ie if they failed to pay the confiscation that was ordered). The confiscation order against Sorelli required £429,010. The order against Szrajber was for £407,188. The amounts were determined based on how much money each defendant received for fixing bids (ie the money that went into the pockets of each).

As soon as the defendants were charged, the police officer responsible gathered information necessary to show that each defendant had enough assets to disgorge the benefits that he derived from his crimes. Each defendant was required to give a statement regarding his finances before the conclusion of the case. The SFO was then given these statements (before the confiscation hearing) so that they could verify the information tendered by the defendants. In this case, the SFO had two weeks to verify the information contained in the affidavit.

In another of the bid rigging cases, defendant East (an insider who divulged information about the awarding company's bidding process) was targeted for confiscation at the time he was charged. Fearing dissipation of his assets, East's assets were restrained from the start (so that the officer would not need to keep telephoning the parties to ensure that the assets were still there). After the order, East was permitted to transfer monies from an Isle of Man account into his lawyer's account in the UK to help with his considerable living expenses. (The orders, being *in personam*, do not have direct effect on institutions that are not under the control of legal and natural persons within the English jurisdiction: so the Isle of Man bank was not constrained by the restraint order. *Inter alia*, unless it is part of the investigation of the crime, if the defendant lies about his assets in overseas accounts, the investigators do not have the power to check this directly.) On sentence, the judge ordered confiscation against East in the amount of £153,765. Since he has not yet completed his prison term, it is unknown whether he will pay this amount. But because the case was now in the prosecution, rather than the investigation, phase, the SFO considered that the court did not have the power to order the banks to produce their records. Thus, even if a court ordered all the moneys in Account X forfeited, it is conceivable that the prosecution would not know how much was in Account X and that if a defendant lied about the amount, there was no way to obtain the documentation to prove or disprove what the defendant represented. However, since case law shows that confiscation matters *are* criminal matters, it seems likely that PACE Production Orders - which relate to information "for the purpose of a criminal investigation" - can be obtained, and in any event, the High Court might deem it within their powers to order disclosure as part of their broad jurisdiction. If a receiver had been appointed, he would have had powers to obtain information in the accounts.

Crime Prevention Unit Series Papers

1. **Reducing Burglary: a study of chemists' shops.** Gloria Laycock. 1985.
2. **Reducing Crime: developing the role of crime prevention panels.** Lorna J.F Smith and Gloria Laycock. 1985.
3. **Property Marking: a deterrent to domestic burglary?** Gloria Laycock. 1985.
4. **Designing for Car Security: towards a crime free car.** Dean Southall and Paul Ekblom. 1986.
5. **The Prevention of Shop Theft: an approach through crime analysis.** Paul Ekblom. 1986.
6. **Prepayment Coin Meters: a target for burglary.** Nigel Hill. 1986.
7. **Crime in Hospitals: diognosis and prevention.** Lorna J.F. Smith.
8. **Preventing Juvenile Crime: the Staffordshire Experience.** Kevin Heal and Gloria Laycock. 1987.
9. **Preventing Robberies at Sub-Post Offices: an evaluation of a security initiative.** Paul Ekblom. 1987.
10. **Getting the Best out of Crime Analysis.** Paul Ekblom. 1988.
11. **Retail Crime: Prevention through Crime Analysis.** John Burrows. 1988.
12. **Neighbourhood Watch in England and Wales: a locational analysis.** Sohail Husain. 1988.
13. **The Kirkholt Burglary Prevention Project, Rochdale.** David Forrester, Mike Chatterton and ken Pease with the assistance of Robin Brown. 1988.
14. **The Prevention of Robbery at Building Society Branches.** Claire Austin. 1988.
15. **Crime Prevention and Racial Harassment in Asian-run Small Shops: the scope for prevention.** Paul Ekblom and Frances Simon with the assistance of Sneh Birdi. 1988.
16. **Crime and Nuisance in the Shopping Centre: a case study in crime prevention.** Susan Phillips and Raymond Cochrane. 1988.
17. **The Prevention of Fraud.** Michael Levi. 1988.
18. **An Evaluation of Domestic Security Surveys.** Gloria Laycock. 1989.
19. **Downtown Drinkers: the perceptions and fears of the public in a city centre.** Malcolm Ramsey. 1989.
20. **The Management and Prevention of Juvenile Crime Problems.** Barrymore Cooper. 1989.
21. **Victim Support and Crime Prevention in an Inner-City Setting.** Alice Sampson and Graham Farrell. 1990.
22. **Largerland Lost? An experiment in keeping Drinkers off the street in cental Coventry and elsewhere.** Malcolm Ramsey. 1990.

23. **The Kirkholt Burglary Prevention Project: Phase II.** David Forrester, Samantha Frenz, Martin O,Connell and Ken Pease. 1990.
24. **Probation Practice in Crime Prevention.** Jane Geraghty. 1991.
25. **Lessons from a Victim Support Crime Prevention Project.** Alice Sampson. 1991.
26. **The Prevention of Cheque and Credit Card Fraud.** Michael Levi, Paul Bissell and Tony Richardson. 1991.
27. **Making Crime Prevention Pay: initiatives from business.** John Burrows. 1991.
28. **The Influence of Street Lighting on Crime and Fear of Crime.** Stephen Atkins, Sohail Husain and Angele Storey. 1991.
29. **The Effect of Better Street Lighting on Crime and Fear: a Review.** Malcolm Ramsay with the assistance of Rosemary Newton. 1991.
30. **Reducing Crime on the London Underground.** Barry Webb and Gloria Laycock. 1992.
31. **Assessing Crime Prevention Initiatives: The First Steps.** Geoff Berry and Mike Carter. 1992.
32. **Tackling Car Crime.** Barry Webb and Gloria Laycock. 1992.
33. **Car Theft in England and Wales: The Home Office Car Theft Index.** George Houghton. 1992.
34. **Preventing Car Crime in Car Parks.** Barry Webb, Ben Brown and Katherine Bennett. 1992.
35. **Closed Circuit Television in Public Places.** Terry Honess and ElizabetCharman. 1992.
36. **Multiple Victimisation: Racial Attacks on an East London Estate.** Alice Sampson and Coretta Phillips. 1992.
37. **Theft and Loss from UK Libraries: A National Survey.** John Burrows and Diane Cooper. 1992.
38. **Safer Cities and Community Safety Strategies.** Nick Tilley. 1992.
39. **Community Service and Crime Prevention: the Cheadle Heath Project.** Mary Barker, Ken Pease and Barry Webb. 1992.
40. **Car Crime and Young People on a Sunderland Housing Estate.** Eileen Spencer. 1993.
41. **Developing Police Crime Prevention: Management and Organisational Change.** Valerie Johnston, Joanna Shapland and Paul Wiles. 1993.
42. **Understanding Car Parks, Crime and CCTV: Evaluation Lessons from Safer Cities.** Nick Tilley. 1993.
43. **Kerb-Crawling, prostitution and Multi-Agency Policing.** Roger Matthews. 1993.

Crime Detection and Prevention Series

POLICE RESEARCH SERIES PAPERS

1. **Video Taping Police Interviews with Suspects - an Evaluation.** John Baldwin. 1992.
2. **Effective Shift Systems for the Police Service.** Richard Stone, Tim Kemp, Bernard Rix and George Weldon. 1993.
3. **Opportunities for Reducing the Administrative Burdens on the Police.** Paul Cresswell, Graham Howarth, Mike Dolan and John Hedges. 1993.
4. **Investigative Interviewing Courses For Police Officers: An Evaluation.** Barry McGurk, Michael Carr and Debra McGurk. 1993.
5. **Management and Supervision of Police Interviews.** Janet Stockdale. 1993.
6. **Royal Commission Research Papers. A Policing Perspective.** Jane Hirst. 1993.
7. **Part-Time Working and Job Sharing in the Police Service.** Richard Stone, Tim Kemp and George Weldon. 1994.
8. **Managing demand on the Police: An evaluation of a Crime Line.** Chloe Jolowicz and Tim Read. 1994.
9. **Court Attendance by Police Officers.** Bob Eames, Andrew Hooke and David Portas. 1994.
10. **Assaults on Police Officers: An examination of the circumstances in which such incidents occur.** Ben Brown. 1994.
11. **Assessing the Expandable Side-handled Baton.** Egmont Koch, Tim Kemp and Bernard Rix. 1994.
12. **Traffic Organisation and Activity Study.** Adam Ogilvie-Smith, Elizabeth Ransom and Alan Downey. 1994.